A Mother's Hilarious Journey from Burn-Out to Glory

NANCY KENNEDY

MULTNOMAH BOOKS • SISTERS, OREGON

MOM ON THE RUN

published by Multnomah Books
a part of the Questar publishing family

© 1996 by Nancy Kennedy

International Standard Book Number: 0-88070-858-1

Cover illustration by John Ceballos
Cover design by David Carlson
Edited by Shari MacDonald

Printed in the United States of America

Most Scripture quotations are from the *New International Version*
©1973, 1984 by International Bible Society
used by permission of Zondervan Publishing House

Also quoted:
The *New American Standard Bible*
©1960, 1977 by the Lockman Foundation; used by permission
The Living Bible (© 1971 by Tyndale House Publishers)
The Revised Standard Version Bible
©1946, 1952, 1971, by the Division of Christian Education of the National Council of the
Churches of Christ in the USA
The King James Version

For information:
QUESTAR PUBLISHERS, INC.
POST OFFICE BOX 1720
SISTERS, OREGON 97759

This is dedicated to my mother,
the best Sugar Plum Fairy
Nevada Avenue Elementary School ever had.

CONTENTS

Acknowledgments

EVEN THOUGH MY name is on the cover, it takes many people to write a book. To my editor and favorite romance novelist, Shari MacDonald, thank you for all your words of encouragement, friendship, and guidance. You're a good sport. Thank you also to Michele Tennesen, David Kopp, Brenda Saltzer, and Blake Weber at Questar, and to Heather Harpham. Cookies all around for these folks!

Cookies also for Tina, Diane, Sue, and Eloise at Books and Bookings for all their hard work in getting me on the radio. Whenever you hear my whiny, nasal voice stammering over the airwaves, you can thank them.

A firm handshake to Ray Cortese, my pastor at Seven Rivers Presbyterian Church, in gratitude for teaching me about God's irresistible grace and for changing his Sunday shirt. (Nice tie, too, Ray.) Thank you also to my entire church family for supporting me and encouraging me to continue writing even though the thought terrifies me. Hugs to you all. May God grant a full night's sleep to each of you with little ones at home. A special howdy to my favorite prankster and fax pal, Jacqui Frazee.

To Mary Ann Fulkerson: Hallelujah, Amen.

My daughters are the delight of my life. Who else would put up with a mother who forgets to pick her own child up after school, tosses the wrong jeans in the dryer, considers thawed frozen peas nature's perfect food, and who cries at reruns of "Full House"? Guess what, guys—I'm the mom God chose for you! All complaints go to Him.

I married a great guy. Except for the ice cream dribbles on the bedspread and that infamous St. Patrick's Day, I don't regret any of the past twenty years. Thank you, Barry, for your patience, good humor, and willingness to kill snakes. You get the Golden Rake Award.

Heavenly Father, all I have accomplished, You have done for me. Your name alone do I honor (Isaiah 26:12-13). May my words be Your words; may all glory go to You.

Introduction

Dear Reader,

Correct me if I'm wrong, but nobody ever says, "When I grow up, I want small children to throw up regularly in my lap and drool on my arm. I want to go without an entire night's sleep for eighteen months straight, have a stomach so flabby I can tuck it into the back pocket of my jeans, and develop an intricate pattern of fine (and not-so-fine) white lines all over my hips, breasts, and belly." Did you ever say that? I didn't think so, and neither did I.

I wanted to be an actress when I grew up. I wanted to be Mary Tyler Moore and work in a newsroom. I wanted to marry Batman and write scripts for his show. I wanted to sing with the Beatles, own a restaurant, be a photojournalist for *Life* magazine, walk a tightrope, and live on a Greek island.

Of course, I didn't exactly have a plan as to how I would do all of that. I just knew I wanted to do something grand and wonderful with my life. Affect the masses, change the world, be somebody important and precious and madly adored. Looking back, it was probably a good thing I didn't have a step-by-step life plan to follow because it seems God already had one. His involved small children throwing up regularly in my lap, drooling on my arm, and keeping me in a constant state of sleep deprivation.

For the past nineteen years I've held the title of Mom. I've changed thousands of diapers, wiped two adorable noses hundreds of times, and sat through scores of softball games. I've eaten the crusts nobody wants, used my shirt to clean off dirty faces, and cried countless tears over a toddler who refused to go in the big potty, and over a ten-year-old who wouldn't eat for a year.

I missed marrying Batman. Instead, I married a man with a bat who could knock a softball out of the park every time he swung and who (with God's blessing) helped me produce two delightful, nerve-wracking bundles of sweetness and cocky attitudes.

As for being Mary Tyler Moore...well, that role has already been taken. I never made it to a newsroom, never sang with the Beatles, and never owned a restaurant. I've lived in the frigid potato fields of northern Maine, fifteen miles down the street from Disneyland, on the fog-entrenched Monterey Bay, and in the woods of central Florida...but never on a Greek island.

I never made it to the stage or movie screen, either, but I *have* walked a tightrope. One has to, in trying to determine what's fair while raising two children who continuously keep score. ("She got to sit in the front seat yesterday." "You bought her gum last week.") And although my photos have yet to make it into *Life* magazine (Who am I kidding? They rarely make it into a photo album!), I have had the privilege of living the life God had planned for me from before the foundation of the world.

Maybe I haven't done anything that seems grand and wonderful. Maybe I haven't affected the masses, changed the world, or become somebody important, precious, and madly adored. Still...my husband loves me, and my daughters—in moments of weakness—tell me I'm OK. (Trust me, coming from teens and preteens, that's the equivalent of a standing ovation or a dozen red roses.)

I'm not the world's greatest mom. I laugh at things I should take seriously and harp on things best left ignored. When Laura was four, I broke her heart by throwing out a treasured coloring book. The year Alison wouldn't eat I hauled her into our pastor's office and cried, "Fix my child!" I can't pitch in the strike zone, and I almost always hide the last Twinkie instead of sharing it. Like I said, I'm not the world's greatest mother. Even so, I have discovered incredible joy and an abundance of laughter during my tenure as the mom of this family.

Jesus posed a paradox to his disciples: Lose your life to find it. I may not have achieved anything on my wish list, but in losing my wants, I found what I needed: a life filled with carpooling, orthodontia, lost jackets, and cheerleading practice four nights a week. It's not a glamorous life, but it's the life God custom-designed just for me.

I wrote this book with two thoughts in mind: to entertain you and to encourage you in whatever stage of motherhood you may find yourself: from baby drool to safety patrol car washes. I can't make the diapers disappear or the chicken pox go away, but I can let you in on a secret: This too shall pass.

In the meantime, whether you're curled up in your favorite chair or reading this in a rare, solitary minute-and-a-half in the bathroom, my prayer is that you'll find laughter and hope within these pages.

Your friend,

Nancy Kennedy

CHAPTER ONE

Confessions of a Runaway Mom

I MUST HAVE looked like a mad woman: five-foot-one-inch of insanity schlepping a worn brown leather suitcase through the crowded airport terminal, stopping every ten feet or so to catch my breath and growl.

Drag, drag, *grrr.* Drag, drag, *errchhhh.*

As I approached the ticket counter and saw the line of would-be travelers snaking through the concourse area, I almost turned around and went home.

Almost.

Then I remembered why I was there. I tugged my sweatshirt over my hips, pushed my sunglasses up on my head, growled again, and schlepped farther.

"They'll be sorry," I muttered. "They're gonna miss me." (*They* being my family: husband and chief chocolate ice cream dribbler of the past twenty years, Barry; oldest daughter, Alison, whose penchant for storing dirty dishes and half-empty Diet Pepsi cans under her bed knows no bounds; and Laura. the daughter who can win at Ms. Pac Man while lying on the floor — with her eyes closed — but who cannot manage to hit the trash can in broad daylight with two hands and both eyes open.)

I growled some more, dragged my suitcase to the end of the line, and sighed. *Free at last, free at last. Thank God Almighty. I'm free at last.*

I still don't know how I ended up at the airport....

I take that back. I know exactly how. I'd been dreaming of this for years. An escape. A leave of absence. An adventure. An extended vacation. Maternal R & R.

It had been building for years, like a game of House of Cards. It started with babies who thought God created nights for parental sleep-deprivation marathons and continued with leg-clinging toddlers whose inquiring minds wanted to know, "Why do you have hair in your nose, Mommy?" "Why does your tummy hang down like that, Mommy?" and "Why don't my legs shake like yours do, Mommy?"

Card by card, incident by incident. It was the preschooler who declared eternal devotion to Big Bird — then when I bought every imaginable Big Bird "must have" on the market, switched her devotion to the Little Mermaid as Big Bird laid an egg. It was standing in incredibly long — and often hostile — lines for a Cabbage Patch doll, and years later, for a blue Power Ranger action figure.

It was all the wails of, "Pick the mushrooms out, Mom!" and "Why *can't* I play handball in my bedroom?" It was the half-eaten Jolly Rancher cinnamon sticks left on the car dashboard, the dirty clothes shoved behind the bathroom door, and the eighty dollar sneakers left out in the rain. It was the constant strains of "I'm telling...She did it...I got here first...I don't wanna...Do I hafta?...She's touching me...She's looking at me...Tell her to leave me alone…Can I stay up just a little longer?…Please, please, please, please, pleeeeeezzzz?"

As I said, it had been building. However, the last straw came the day before my escape. I'd been lying on the kitchen floor trying unsuccessfully to fish Laura's report card out from under the refrigerator using an opened paper clip and a wad of gum. I had barbecue sauce on my chin and down the front of my bathrobe. This was from an earlier attempt at carrying a plastic baggie of leftover chicken in my mouth while using one hand to sign a field trip permission slip and the other to swat at the cat, who was on the kitchen counter licking mayonnaise out of the jar. At ten o'clock in the morning, I still hadn't taken a shower, brushed my teeth, opened my Bible, or glanced at the morning paper. I had what my kids call "bed head," where one side of my hair sticks straight up and the other side sort of smashes against my face. Also, although I wasn't sure what it was — or if I even wanted to know — I had something squishy between my toes.

As I hobbled over to the kitchen sink to rinse off my feet, the washing machine started squealing and bouncing around the laundry room. The phone rang. The dryer buzzer went off. The Pest Control guy knocked at the door to inform me I had a grain beetle infestation. Seven new wrinkles spontaneously embedded themselves onto my face and the extra five pounds I'd been carrying around on my body for the past fifteen years suddenly tripled.

I shut off the washer and yelled at the dryer to go make its bed. I answered the phone, "The party you have reached is no longer functioning as a human being. She has been disconnected. Her circuits have crossed. Please hang up and go clean your room."

I handed the Pest Control guy a brown-bag lunch and a pile of clean undershirts, told him the toilet in the hall kept running, and asked him to pick up some light bulbs at the store on his way home. I'm not sure, but I think I may even have kissed him good-bye.

I spent the rest of the day — still in my barbecue sauce-stained bathrobe — watching game shows and reruns of "The Love Boat," drinking chocolate Yoo Hoo's, and daydreaming of a carefree life somewhere else. I imagined myself, toned and tanned, with hands not smelling of tile cleaner, lolling on a white sandy beach in the absence of kids screaming, "I'm telling!" or "You are *so* a doofus brain!"

By the time the girls came home — Alison from classes at the community college and Laura from middle school — I'd drunk myself into a chocolate stupor. They found me in the living room with the blinds drawn and lights off, curled up in my brown armchair, swaying my head and chanting, "I'd like to buy a vowel, please!"

But I hadn't lost it completely.

Not yet, anyway.

I told the girls I'd been rehearsing a part in a play about a woman who loses her identity somewhere between 2:00 A.M. feedings and chaperoning fifth grade safety patrollers to Washington, D.C., and who ends up conversing with squirrels and collecting wire bread ties. They looked at me as if I'd spoken Greek and shook their heads.

"A mind is a terrible thing to waste," Alison quipped, then turned to her sister. "If I ever get senile like that, just shoot me."

As they laughed and went in the kitchen to scatter crumbs on the counters and splash iced tea on the cupboards, I dragged myself from my chair and went to take a shower.

The rest of the day and evening was a blur. I vaguely remember quizzing Laura on prepositions and the life cycle of plants. Someone with a five o'clock shadow kissed me hello (I'm assuming it was Barry and not the Pest Control guy), and I think I solved a major crisis of Alison's regarding whether or not she should wear her light blue jeans or her dark blue ones the next day.

The details are fuzzy. What I *do* remember clearly is the mustard.

It was a couple of hours after dinner. Barry was out in the backyard watering the lawn, and the girls had assumed their usual evening positions: Alison, holed up in her room, "studying," with a steady, migraine-inducing female voice yodeling about zombies, booming from her CD player; and Laura, lying on her back in the dining room, her feet on the wall, the telephone surgically attached to her head. As she talked (I take that back — she and her friends rarely talk while on the phone, they just lie there on permanent hold), she watched a line of ants march up the kitchen counter and across the sink, then converge on a puddle of melted ice cream leaking from a carton somebody forgot to put away.

As maddening as all that may have been (not to mention my ire at finding, a few moments earlier, a freshly laundered pile of clothes back in the laundry hamper — still folded), the mustard proved to be the card that toppled the house.

I don't know what it is about mustard. I don't want it that often, but when I do — it's never there. That particular night, I'd gotten through dinner with some semblance of normalcy (Thank You, Lord, for home delivery pizza), gotten through wiping shaving cream splatters off the bathroom mirror and washing out the cats' food dishes. I'd kicked a path through the maze of school books and assorted shoes scattered in the entry way and had grabbed a half-dozen empty shampoo bottles out of the shower — my usual evening activities.

On my way back from the trash can in the garage, I realized I was still hungry. I knew what would hit the spot: a slice of ham, open-faced on a lightly toasted piece of rye bread with a dollop of mustard. That's all I wanted. A ham sandwich with mustard. Just a dollop.

A dollop.

When I reached the kitchen — my taste buds set on my after-dinner snack — the House of Cards crashed at my feet. The jar of mustard — *my* mustard — lay on the kitchen floor with a note on it that read, "Be careful — broken glass."

Now, my opinion is: If you're old enough to write a note, you're old enough to clean up the mess. However, no one else in the family subscribed to that theory. They'd long since adopted the "let Mom do it" school of thought.

Well, right then and there, Mom decided she wasn't going to "do it" any longer. I calmly stepped over the broken jar, calmly stepped over Laura, thought twice about ripping the phone off the wall, then calmly — without my slice of ham, without my lightly toasted rye bread, and without my dollop of mustard — I announced, "Good night, everyone; I'm going to bed."

But I didn't go to bed. Instead, I pulled a trusty, old, brown leather suitcase (given to me by my own mom) down from the closet shelf. I blew off the dust and pried the rusty locks open, then stuffed it with mismatched clothes, several pairs of shoes, the Raggedy Ann doll my aunt gave me my first Christmas away from home and — in a moment of temporary insanity — the TV remote control.

"Now they're really going to miss me!" I gloated and threw all my weight on top of my suitcase as it strained to stay closed.

Little did my family suspect they weren't going to have ol' Mom to kick around any more — at least for a while. It wasn't until the next morning when I grabbed my stash of mad money from the back of my underwear drawer — and if this wasn't a moment of madness, I don't know what is — got on the Florida turnpike and headed for the Orlando airport that I realized exactly what I'd done.

I'd become…a mom on the run.

CHAPTER TWO

I Am Mommy, Hear Me Roar

HE TURNED AROUND and smiled at me, almost as if I were human. I was only one hour into my runaway adventure, and already people were starting to notice me as more than just a duster of ceiling fans and breader of pork chops.

The man's blue eyes gazed into my olive green ones, and he opened his mouth to speak.

"Lady," he said, "you're standing on my magazine."

Mumbling an embarrassed "Oops, sorry," I bent over, dusted off the 'Q' on his GQ, and handed it back to him. Then, adjusting my position in line, I focused my attention on the several hundred thousand travel destinations from which I had to choose. I scanned the computerized listing as one would look over a flavor menu at an ice cream parlor. *If you can't decide among thirty-one ice cream choices, how do you expect to choose one of a zillion places to go?* taunted a voice inside my head.

"I'll decide when I get up to the counter," I answered.

In the line ahead of me, Blue Eyes moved several steps forward while the surrounding travelers stared as if they'd never seen a woman talking to herself before.

I shrugged and continued my conversation with myself.

You're crazy. You know that, don't you? You can't just run away. Moms don't run away, said my inner voice.

"I'm not crazy," I said aloud, looking exactly that. "Every mom thinks about running away at times. Besides, I just want to go where God can use my talents and gifts. Someplace glorious. Someplace where I'm loved and appreciated and where it's not my fault if it rains and a camping trip gets canceled."

Sounds great. Where is that?

"That's the problem. I don't know."

By the time I'd finished my conversation, I had reached the head of the line. There, a chipper young man with a full thirty-two-tooth grin greeted me from behind the counter. He had All-American, Rah-Rah, Ivy League, Mom, and Apple Pie written all over him.

"Hello! I'm Blake!" he said and clicked his pen. "Do you have any reservations?" he asked — still grinning, still clicking his pen.

I wrinkled my brow. Reservations? Well, maybe a few. Depending on how long I'd be gone, I might miss Laura's softball tryouts or my annual Christmas shopping trip with Alison, where I show her what I like, she tells Barry, and he buys it.

It's not that I don't love them. It's just....

And then there's Barry and the spare room we're working on....

But then there's the fighting and the whining and the bickering and the tripping over work boots and the....

"Nope. No reservations," I told Blake and pounded the counter. "I'm gonna do this. Just write me up a ticket."

His smile didn't change one iota. He simply raised his left eyebrow and said, "O — kay. What's your name, ma'am?"

"My name?" Suddenly, my mind went blank. It wasn't as if I didn't know my own name. I just didn't know which one to give him.

Mommy? Mom? Mama? MomcanIgetmynavelpierced? MomIthinkI'mgonnathrowup? A long time ago, I gave up using the name on my birth certificate and just started referring to myself as Mommy. As in:

"Come give Mommy a kiss."

"Tell Mommy where it hurts."

"I told you Mommy's ears can't hear whining."

"Mommy's face looks like this because Mommy just found out that somebody used her lace tablecloth to wipe off fingernail polish."

I knew I wasn't alone on that either. I know for a fact that none of my friends have names. We greet each other in the market:

"Hi, Sarah's mom!"

"Hi, Laura's mom!"

The vet even calls me "Blackie's mom."

At one women's luncheon where I was introduced as "Nancy Kennedy," I simply sat in my seat, looking around, until the woman next to me discreetly pointed to my name tag and whispered, "That's you!"

That's why I hesitated at Blake's seemingly simple request. There was nothing simple about my name or the awesome responsibility it carried.

"Mom," I told him. "My name is Mom."

He wrinkled his brow and scratched his head. "I'm sorry, but the company needs more than just 'Mom.' Do you have another name?"

It was my turn to wrinkle my brow and scratch my head.

"Another name?" I echoed. I was about to tell him that Barry sometimes calls me Honey or Sweetheart (although more often "Where'd you put my_____"), when Blake interrupted my thoughts.

"Do you have a credit card with your name on it?" he suggested, then told me firmly: "We need to know who you are."

Who am I? You know who I am. There's a container of Gak dumped in a corner of my living room carpet and the moldy remains of a peach deemed too gross to eat stuffed in the cushions of my couch. I walk around the house with dryer lint and used Q-tips in the pocket of my robe. I spend the majority of my day behind the wheel of a car — traveling hundreds of miles to and from softball practice, cheerleading practice, and trips to the market — yet never leave the city limits. I can't do a quadratic equation, but I can tell you how to get to Sesame Street.

My prayers are often frantic and generally specific. ("Lord, please help my child throw up in the bucket and not on the wall.") At times I pray to be made invisible, like during PTA meetings when they need someone to chair the fifth grade fundraising car wash or during the Christmas program when it's my child up on stage singing, "Let there be peace on earth and let it begin with me," as she proceeds to slug the boy standing next to her.

I know you know me. I wash my children's faces with spit and my thumb. Pick at the dirt behind their ears. Whine about their whining. Nag about their nagging. Worry that I'll never live to see the day they'll change their underwear without coercion or threats of bodily harm.

I have eyes in the back of my head and a nose that can sniff out doggy doo-doo on a sneakered foot fifty yards away. I have ears that can hear Oreo cookies being eaten underneath the covers by a child who is supposedly asleep. With just one sideways glance, I can tell who sharpened her crayon with my eyeliner pencil sharpener and who accidentally-on-purpose let the bathroom sink overflow.

A few years ago, you would have recognized me as the one with strained chicken and peas plastered in my hair and a faraway look in my eyes, as I dreamed of a life that was not planned around nap time and late night feedings. I was the one who, when asked by a poll-taker to name my favorite male television performer, answered without hesitation, "Ernie from Sesame Street."

Once upon a time I had a stomach that didn't fall to the floor. Once, I had hips that didn't serve as a baby saddle and a shelf for grocery bags. Once, I could even take a bath. Alone. All by myself. Without someone pounding on the closed door, asking if she could use the blue food coloring or "just wondering" if Super Glue ruins dining room tables.

If you looked in my closet you'd find baggy sweats with elastic waists; big, long sweaters; and pull-on pants. Forget Bill Blass and Anne Klein, give me Hanes Her Way any day.

You know who I am. I eat standing up. "Breakfast" consists of the soggy cereal left in bowls on the kitchen table, the ends of bread left in the bag, and blobs of strawberry jam scraped from the counter. I grab lunch on the run from a drive-through window and nibble on dinner as I cook it. I finish everyone else's ice cream, then wonder why I can't ever seem to lose weight.

Don't tell anyone, but I live for bedtime. I yearn for the sounds of a child's slumber. I long for my own head to hit the pillow. I pine for (yawn)...zzzzz.

You know me. I'm the one with the knot in her stomach, praying her child will figure out how to turn over on the playground turnover bar so she won't be humiliated in front of her classmates during gym class. I'm the one who drinks the powdered milk so the rest of the family can have the "real" stuff. I'm the one who eagerly counted the days until both daughters went to school, then cried when that day finally arrived.

I'm the one who willingly suffered through morning sickness, swollen ankles, uncontrollable crying jags, and overwhelming desires for lemon meringue pie and out-of-season blackberries. (Not to mention pushing a bowling ball through a part of my body a bowling ball doesn't normally fit — twice.)

I'm the one frightened voices call for in the middle of the night. I'm the one who changes wet sheets at three in the morning, rocks a nightmare-stricken preschooler back to sleep at four, then gets up at five to let the dog out.

I'm the one who, despite an utterly selfish nature and a propensity toward evil (in addition to an inadequacy in and of myself and a definite lack of experience), God chose as caretaker, teacher, and nurturer for two totally dependent little sinners.

With apologies to the Peace Corps, I have the toughest job anyone will ever love. I am battle-weary from refereeing squabbles over who did or did not do the dishes last and battle-scarred from getting smacked in the thigh by a line-driven softball during backyard batting practice. Still, I endure.

Who am I? I am a cooker of oatmeal and cleaner of soap scum. A taxi driver, spider killer, purchaser of folders with pockets and prongs, pencil finder, and dental appointment maker. Loudest cheerleader and most fervent pray-er, encourager of dreams and holder of hands. I am a tear wiper and boo-boo kisser, the toothbrushing gestapo and an example of faith. You know who I am.

I am a mother.

And I don't need a credit card to prove it.

"He settles the barren woman in her home as a happy mother of children" (Psalm 113:9).

Shake, Rattle, and Push

"HELLO?" BLAKE FANNED me with a travel guide pamphlet in an attempt to get my attention. "I need your name, ma'am."

"Well, of course you do — and you'll get it just as soon as I remember it."

I held my purse with my teeth and searched my pockets for my credit card. "I ow I ad id wif me en I lef dis ornin'." Letting my purse drop to the floor, I repeated, "I know I had it with me when I left this morning. Are you sure you can't just put 'Mom'?"

Blake's smile revealed the results of years spent brushing with the nation's leading brand of cavity-fighting toothpaste. "I already told you, the company frowns on it. Why don't you think it over while I help someone else?"

I sighed and kept looking for a hint — any hint. I'd been called Mom for so long....

The irony is, it was never my heart's desire to be a mother. I'm much too selfish for that. Actually, I became a mother quite by surprise. I don't know how I missed the clues: the swollen breasts, the need for a revolving door on the bathroom at night, the hysterical sobbing the time Barry brought home Extra Crispy chicken after I *specifically* asked for Original Recipe.

Then there was the night we went out to dinner with some friends from Boston. That evening, Barry, Frank, and Ann slurped down bucket after bucket of slimy, slithery, steamed clams and plates of raw oysters, dumping each disgusting piece in hot, gritty broth. Then — not content to merely eat it — they dangled every globby, jelly-like, smelly bit in my face.

"Are you sure you don't want any?" one of them would ask. "You don't know what you're missing."

Meanwhile, I wore a path into the restaurant carpeting, making several dozen beelines to the ladies' room while begging God to let me die right then and there. Even after all that, I *still* didn't put two and two together.

It wasn't until the day I went for my annual check up (and to discuss my recent bout of indigestion) that the possibility of a baby even entered my mind.

"What do you think about babies?" the doctor asked from the rather personal side of the paper drape across my knees.

Babies? In our circle of friends we occasionally talked about them in a generic sort of way ("You going to have any?" "Probably someday, I guess."), but no one actually owned one. I vaguely remembered my mom having two or three after I was born, and I distinctly remember flushing my youngest brother's cloth diaper down the toilet and jamming up the plumbing. Other than that, I'd never had any experience with a real, live baby.

But it seemed I was about to…and by the doctor's calculations, my experience would begin in approximately six months. To celebrate, I went out to buy my unborn prodigy a little blue dress (covering both gender bases) and plan how I'd break the news to Barry.

After an afternoon of meticulous plotting, I had it planned down to the last detail. Barry would come in from work and find me, awash in my estrogen-enhanced pregnant glow, nestled in my favorite easy chair while knitting teeny, tiny pink and blue booties. As always, he'd kiss me on top of my head and ask, "How was your day?" I'd smile and keep knitting. Then, when he'd ask about dinner, I'd smile even bigger and inform him: "Tonight's menu will be *baby* carrots, *baby* back ribs, and zwieback biscuits to teethe on for dessert."

I imagined him doing a double take, then asking, "Does this mean what I think it means?" Before I could answer, he'd whisk me off my feet and lift me high in the air. We'd both laugh — then cry — and dance around the room together, singing: "We're having a baby! We're having a baby!"

Well, take away the easy chair, the teeny tiny booties, the carrots, the ribs, and top-of-the-head kiss. While you're at it, take away Barry lifting me high in the air, the laughing (and the crying), and the dancing, too. Now you have the real story of how I broke the news of our pregnancy to my husband.

The real story goes like this: I burned the ribs and over-boiled the carrots, so I had to make do with a half-pound of hamburger, a jar of sauerkraut, and leftover angel food cake. Not only that, Barry couldn't walk in on me knitting because (1) I can't knit and (2) I had the car — a rental car at that, since ours was in the repair shop — and I had to pick him up.

I plotted a back-up plan while driving to the air force supply warehouse where Barry worked. He looked so cute in his green fatigue uniform and his blue baseball hat (the one that had been run over a few too many times by the ton-and-a-half truck he drove)!

As he swept the warehouse floor, I tried to think of something witty and/or endearing to say or do. Finally, I came up from behind and tapped him on the shoulder.

I was about to blurt out, "Hi, Daddy!" Instead, it came out: "I-I-I...um, um, um. The mechanic assured me this time the windshield won't leak. It'll be ready, for sure, this afternoon." I followed him around the warehouse for a few seconds, trying to speak but only swallowing air. Finally, I blurted it out: "I'm, um....I'm, *you know.*"

He didn't know. My pregnant glow had turned to sweat and dripped down my cheek. I tried again. "Barry, I'm —"

"You're *not.*" He threw down the broom he was using and turned to face me. "How did this happen?" he demanded to know.

I gulped. This was not in the script.

"Didn't you deposit that check I gave you?" he continued.

"Yeah, last week, but — "

"But, nothing! How could you be overdrawn again?"

"Barry, I'm not overdrawn. I'm pregnant!"

This time it was his turn to stammer. He hugged me until I thought I'd squish, and squawked out, "I can't believe it! I can't believe it!" After that, he asked his supervisor for the rest of the day off so we could go off to digest the news that one plus one was about to equal three.

The next day was our first anniversary. We just knew we were the first people on earth to ever have a first anniversary and a first baby on the way. To celebrate, we drove to the coastal town of Bar Harbor, Maine. We ate lobster and corn on the cob, then went back to our hotel room to do what every young couple does on their first anniversary.

However, we had a problem. Since we were the first people to ever have a first baby, we didn't know if Marital Bonding would shake up the baby's brains. Barry was the first to bring up the subject.

"What if we shouldn't be doing this?" He jumped off the bed, where we had been kissing. He chewed on his thumbnail and paced the floor.

"Well, I know it's legal," I tried assuring him. My pregnancy hormones were also working overtime, assuring *me* that, yes, not only was it legal, it was also moral and God-ordained — and very much desired.

Still...we were the first people to ever experience this dilemma, and it just might have been true that Marital Bonding does, indeed, shake up a baby's brains. We leafed through all the hotel literature but found nothing to confirm or refute our fears. (After all, we were the first....) Finally, we called the nearest obstetrician to inquire — hypothetically, of course — of Bonding's brain-shaking potential. After a brief chuckle, the doctor prescribed that the two of us go directly to bed and remain there the entire weekend.

We'd never enjoyed following doctor's orders more.

After that, the pregnancy continued as described in all the books. My moods swung. My ankles swelled. I fell asleep in the ladies' room of the air force commissary and woke myself up with my snoring. I discovered that a pregnant belly makes a dandy snack tray and often used mine to hold bowls of ice cream, plates of cheese and crackers, and entire six packs of soda as Barry and I watched TV late at night (saving us numerous trips to and from the kitchen).

Over the course of the six months in which we knew about

Little Alison or Baby Charlie (yes, *Charlie*), we increased our vocabulary with words like effacement, placenta, dilation, and mucous plug. We waited with Great Expectation for the day our vocabulary words would apply to real life. We practiced short, puffy breathing while watching football on TV and took deep cleansing breaths after every meal.

We dreamed and planned for B-Day (Baby Day) to arrive. Yet when it did, it took us completely by surprise.

I'd had a hard day. All I wanted to do was flop on the couch and watch television. But gravity — or whatever it is that tells your body, "It's time!" — won out. As I flopped, my water broke, which signaled the need for us to shut off the television and to try to remember our names and the route to the hospital.

We remembered and made it there in time for a game of "Just Where Is That Doctor?" and six hours of one of us crying to go home and forget the whole thing.

And I wasn't feeling too hot, either.

At the beginning of the seventh hour, the bowling ball decided to make its entrance into the world. That's about the time one of its parents decided he felt faint. As the pushing parent strained to turn her body inside out, the faint-feeling parent announced he might do better out in the hall — to which the pushing parent responded with dangerous-sounding threats muttered through clenched teeth.

The faint parent stayed and watched the birth of his first-born while face-down on the floor of the delivery room, a bottle of smelling salts at his side. It was not the stuff of novels or dreams, but when we held our much-wanted and already-loved daughter, time stood still, heaven rejoiced, and God smiled at the miracle He'd just performed.

After that, Barry and I sighed with relief.
The baby's brains had not been shaken after all.

"Behold, children are a gift of the LORD; The fruit of the womb is a reward" (Psalm 127:3 NASB).

CHAPTER FOUR

They Shoot Polyester, Don't They?

NICE MEMORIES, I thought as I stood at the airport counter, *but now that cute little baby and her sister are both taller than me. Right now they're probably plotting new and improved ways of bringing their sibling rivalry to its highest art form.* I stuffed back my creeping pangs of nostalgia (or was it guilt?) and reminded myself that — temporarily unencumbered by children or the pressures of momdom — I was about to escape to some exotic, glorious place. All I had to do was choose one.

When it was my turn once again, I handed Blake the credit card that identified me as Nancy Kennedy and not "Mom."

Still smiling, he wiggled his eyebrows and said, "Now that we took care of that pesky little bit of info, all I need is your destination."

I went down the "menu" one more time. "I don't know, what do you suggest?" I asked him. "How about something light, yet airy, with a hint of mystery and intrigue thrown in? Someplace not too warm and not too cold. Someplace romantic, but not too romantic. I am a married woman, you know. I just want to go someplace…glorious."

With the patience and enthusiasm of a telemarketer attempting to sell a refrigerator to an Eskimo, Blake suggested, "You're in luck — this month we're having a special on flights to Borneo."

"Borneo?" I wrinkled my nose and shook my head. "Isn't that the place where women wear bones in their noses and they boil strangers in iron pots?"

He scratched his head for a moment. "Hmmm, I don't think so." He clicked his pen half-a-dozen times and scanned his computer monitor for another option. "Vienna?"

I cringed and pounded my chest. "Ugh. Their sausages keep me up all night."

"Bermuda?"

"No. Don't like their shorts."

I found something wrong with every destination he mentioned. My *español* was less than *bueno*, ruling out Spain, South America, and Mexico. My French consisted of *"J'aime beaucoup des haricots"* ("I'm quite fond of beans"), and I didn't think I could get through Paris relying on that.

Blake eyed me somewhat suspiciously. "I don't mean to be rude," he said, "but are you sure you want to go somewhere?"

"Well, of course I'm sure!" I informed him, then pulled out my mad money: $601. I'd been stashing away a dollar a week for the past nineteen years (ever since Alison spit up all over my suede jacket, leaving a permanent stain in the shape of Snoopy).

Minus the $312 I used to replace the motor mount on my car and the $75 for a speeding ticket that was technically not my fault

(I had ice cream in the car that needed a freezer — fast), $601 was all the money I had for my madcap escape.

Somehow it had seemed like a lot more when I left the house that morning.

"I don't mean to be picky," I said, "but I'd rather keep it cheap. What do you have for under two hundred dollars?"

Just then I heard a collective groan from the fifty people standing in line behind me. "Maybe I'll just step aside," I said as somebody flung my suitcase out into the concourse. "I'll come back when I make up my mind."

I chased down my suitcase and dragged it around the lobby for awhile, running up quite a thirst. I was roaming the airport searching for a water fountain, when I saw HIM: a twentyish, blond, pony-tailed Adonis in worn jeans and a white T-shirt. Carrying a worn brown suitcase much like mine, he approached with a smile.

My heart pounded as I ran my fingers through my graying brown hair and tried desperately to will myself twenty pounds thinner. *Not that it matters how I look, technically. I have no intention of leading him on. After all, I may be temporarily AWOL, but I still love my husband. I'll just have to find a gentle way to break Adonis's heart.*

Adonis smiled. As he turned, his eyes lit up. He tossed his head, flexed his biceps…and made his way straight toward me.

As he got closer, I heard him gasp.

"Oh, I'm sorry!" he said. "From a distance, you looked just like my mother. I'm supposed to meet her here."

His mother! Forget the water. I needed something stronger. I needed a cup of coffee.

I found my way to the airport coffee kiosk, and just as I sat down at a table with a cup of the day's brew, I saw HER. Not

Adonis's mother, but...my future.

She walked past me swathed in navy blue polyester. Her strand of imitation pearls matched her clip-on earrings, which matched the color of her hair. Sort of. I could tell by her *eeek-eeek-eeek* that she wore crepe-soled shoes. Comfortable. Sensible.

I wouldn't have paid so much attention to her if it hadn't been for my earlier dialogue with myself and the conversation taking place at the table next to mine.

The two young women were apparently discussing a mutual friend of theirs. They caught my attention when one of them leaned over and said to the other, "She's almost *forty!*"

The other woman gasped, "No! *Really?* You'd never know it — she looks so good."

I nearly choked on my coffee. I'm forty! As far as I was concerned, they were talking about me.

Just then, the lady in blue polyester *eeek-eeeked* her way past my table, briefly patting my hands as if to say: "Your time will come. You'll be one of us someday."

As I sipped my coffee, I started thinking about aging in general — and *my* aging in particular. It didn't seem possible that I had teenagers when only yesterday I was one myself.

I still wear "cool" clothes. My jeans are fashionably faded and properly cuffed (fashion tips courtesy of my daughters). I "slouch" my socks and wear name-brand sneakers. Polyesterville's still a long way off. Except....

Now, don't tell anyone, but last year I started buying pull-on jeans instead of the kind with zippers. I know that means I'm inching toward full polyesterization, but I'm still a long way off. My jeans are still faded and cuffed. Still denim (not, I repeat, *not* you-know-what). It's just that the pull-on kind have a smidge more room. They don't leave holes in my stomach or inhibit normal breathing.

But it's not just clothes. Little things creep their way into every part of life. Speech, for instance. Polyester People talk to their kids about the olden days. "When I was a girl," they say. Lately, I've been saying things like, "I remember thirty years ago...."

Just last week Laura informed me that I was four entire decades old. "That's four. Entire. Decades," she repeated — several times.

But that wasn't what bothered me. It was my *tsk-tsking* at her for saying it that bothered me. Bothered me big time. My mom *tsk-tsks*. My aunt *tsk-tsks*. I've always been a *tsk-tskee*. Now I'm a *tsk-tsker*. Scary, isn't it?

Here are more scary thoughts: I'm old enough to have a husband going through a mid-life crisis. I have friends who can't remember the day President Kennedy was shot — because they weren't even born yet. I have one friend who was only five the year I got married.

I have stray chin whiskers just like the hundred-year-old Russian peasant women in *National Geographic*.

Another frightening thing I've noticed lately is that whenever I go to Wal-Mart, I drift over to the beauty section to look at the anti-aging creams and potions, the exfoliants, and the rejuvenating lotions. I haven't purchased any yet, but I want to. It's just a matter of time...and that scares me.

Even scarier is the growing list of things I'm too old for.

I'm too old to shop at my daughters' favorite store. The last time I shopped there I came home with a pair of overall shorts. For the record, I looked adorable in them. But the one and only time I wore them, I felt conspicuous. Like in my dreams where I'm in a public place and suddenly I realize I'm not wearing a shirt.

I'm too old for overall shorts.

I'm too old for certain words like "duh" and phrases such as "way cool." I can still say "cool" and get away with it, but "way cool" is definitely out.

I also can't call teenage boys "dudes" anymore. Not since they started calling *my* house asking for *my* daughters.

Alas, I'm too old for today's teen idols. Dylan and Brandon from "Beverly Hills 90210" are too young, yet my childhood heroes — David Cassidy, Mickey Dolenz, and Bobby Sherman — are all old men.

Ernie Douglas and Opie Taylor are balding.

The Fonz is gray.

The other day I got a phone call from my friend Karen who lives in California. Of all the things we could have talked about, we discussed the benefits of taking hormone supplements transdermally and wondered whether or not alpha hydroxy lotions can work miracles on our aging faces.

The other day the girls found my old eight-track tape deck in the garage. Laura asked, "Wow, Mom. Is that, like, an antique or something?"

I've had to explain skate keys to them. Describe platform shoes and window pane tights. Pixie haircuts and *puka* shell necklaces.

We're talking major generation gap stuff. And — like middle-age spread — it's getting wider.

They like *loud* rock music. I prefer easy-listening. Quiet. Soothing. Good ol' Barry Manilow.

They like killer roller coaster rides. I like a brisk sit on a bench where I can watch.

They can eat corn dogs *and* Rice Krispie marshmallow treats *and* drink Coca Cola Classic right before bedtime. I consider my cup of Sanka and bran muffin living dangerously.

They think it's fun to stay up late. (Here's an observation about the concept of "late." The older one gets, the earlier "late" becomes. These days, Barry and I usually start nodding off before the girls are tucked in. In fact, they often tuck *us* in.)

His mother. He thinks I look like his mother. I took another sip of coffee and sighed. Then I laughed. *So you look and feel your age — you're supposed to. It's not a crime. Besides, hasn't God said, "Even to your old age and gray hairs I am he, I am he who will sustain you"?* (Isaiah 46:4).

"They will still bear fruit in old age, they will stay fresh and green, proclaiming, 'The LORD is upright; he is my Rock'" (Psalm 92:14-15).

CHAPTER FIVE

I Have Met the Enemy, and It Is... Ring around the Collar

IT'S ONE THING to run away from something; it's quite another to have a place to run to. I still didn't have a clue as to my destination. I wasn't looking for much. Just a place where tape dispensers never run out or end up under somebody's bed, where cereal remains in the box and not scattered across the floor or pushed under the stove, where refrigerators are used to store food and not as hiding places for math homework, and where nobody wakes me up to tell me they can't sleep. I wanted to go where nobody laughed when I sang the score from *Evita* while doing dishes and where I could close the bathroom door without having to account for how long I'd be in there...or if I was ever coming out.

I finished my coffee and tossed out my cup, picked up my

suitcase, and got back to the business at hand: running away.

"How about Albuquerque, New Mexico?" suggested Blake when I reached the front of the ticket line again. "It's sunny and the desert flowers are spectacular in the mornings. I've heard it's glorious. That's what you said you're looking for, isn't it? Glory?"

"Well, that sounds good, but I refuse to go anyplace I can't spell without using a dictionary." That canceled out Irondequoit and Canandaigua, New York; Okeechobee and Chattahoochee, Florida; and Connecticut. Also Massachusetts, most European cities, half of the African continent, and all of Asia.

I mentally scanned the list of places I could spell and had just opened my mouth to say, "L.A.," when an ink stain on the pocket of Blake's white shirt caught my eye. I may have been running away from home, but I'd yet to shake the "mom" in me. Something snapped. My eyes clouded over and I began reciting all the laundry laws I'd memorized over the past twenty years.

"Hairspray takes out pen marks."

"No bleach on Lycra."

"Wash colors separately."

"Empty all living animals out of jeans pockets before starting the wash cycle."

It really was second nature. I'd spent years scrubbing bicycle chain grease out of white leggings, lamenting over blue jeans that keep shrinking, bemoaning Dry Clean Only tags on sweaters that enter the dryer adult-sized and emerge Barbie doll-sized, and sighing as I pretreated pizza sauce on white blouses (that, let's face it, despite commercial promises, would *never* come out).

As I leafed through a magazine the other day, I came across a laundry detergent advertisement that depicted a mountain of towels on a bathroom floor and a towel-clad body tossing another one on the pile. The caption read: "It's like I wash towels for a small nation."

Can I get an "Amen," sister? Here's the deal: Daughter A takes a shower. She needs a towel for her body and one for her hair. When she's done, she drops her two wet (yet not dirty) towels somewhere in the vicinity of the laundry room. Next, Daughter B takes a shower. She needs three towels: one for her body, one for her head, and one to wipe up the water left on the floor from her younger sister, who hasn't yet figured out the correlation between leaving the shower curtain open and the subsequent ankle-deep puddles on the floor. (She's also the one who snuck out of bed one night and watched *Psycho* without parental approval, yet insists her preference for wide-open showers has nothing to do with the movie's shower/murder scene. That it began shortly after she saw the movie is purely coincidental.)

Ever since Eve told Adam, "It's not dirty, it's only wet!" wives and mothers have spent precious, yet wasted, words trying to get their families to hang up wet towels. My mother had to contend with no less than eight each day. Each day, like a broken record, she'd stand at the foot of the stairs with her arms full of drippy bath towels and say, "They're not dirty; they're just wet. Go hang them up."

I confess: When Mom started obsessing about wet towels and the never-ending piles of dirty and barely dirty clothes ("Mom, you can't expect me to hang up something I wore for a whole minute and a half!"), I'd roll my eyes and think, *What's the big deal? It's only laundry.* Little did I know, laundry is not "only laundry."

I know better now.

I am a mother. Laundry is my foe. It is something one "tackles." It is to be seized and conquered, brought into submission.

It's boring and mundane. The only laundry-related fun I've ever had was the time when, as children, my brothers and I took my sister to the Laundry Land Laundromat and put her in the dryer. We told her Mom said she could go on the Tilt-O-Whirl next time the carnival came around, and that this was good practice for her.

One brother held down the button that tells the dryer the door's shut, my other brother put the money in, and I turned the machine on. Peggy spun a few times but got scared and made us stop — which we were about to do anyway after seeing the Laundromat lady coming at us, shaking her wire coat hanger and advising us not to come back.

Then there was the time I mistakenly used swimming pool chlorine for bleach (bleach — chlorine, they're the same thing, right?) and ended up with a hole the size of Lake Superior in my mom's white linen tablecloth. Thankfully, I managed to patch it with lace doilies that (*whew!*) made it look like an heirloom antique.

Aside from that and the Spinning Sister episode, laundry has been less than thrilling for me. Especially when I'm the one more or less (OK, OK, more) responsible for making sure everyone in the family has at least two clean socks that match (more or less) each morning.

I have this recurring dream in which I'm buried under a pile of dirty clothes, struggling desperately to claw my way to the top. Every time I get a glimpse of daylight, someone yells, "Oops! Does cranberry juice stain?" and a truckload of juice-splattered white T-shirts is downloaded onto my face.

It starts when they're babies. (Laundry Lamentation #1: The smaller the person, the bigger the pile of laundry.) First they spit up on everything. When they outgrow that, they drool. When they stop drooling, they eat spaghetti with their hands and mistake the front of their Oshkosh's for their mouth.

Once their aim gets a bit more accurate and they start using spoons as something other than a tool for dumping mashed potatoes in their lap, children toddle outside and discover that mud pies bake better in the sun when they are first placed upon a jacket or a sweater on the ground. After that, they discover that pockets are best for storing Play-Doh, shirttails work better than tissues for a runny nose, and pizza can only be eaten after it's dumped on a white T-shirt.

That's the stage my family's at currently. Once, after not being able to take one more, "Oops! Does _____ stain?" I actually yelled, "From now on, *nobody* is allowed to eat with their clothes on!"

In all my years of unrolling wet, muddy socks; handling gym clothes left all weekend in a backpack until Sunday night; and discovering mountains of rapidly mildewing damp bath towels that have been stuffed way back in someone's closet, I've observed a few indisputable and undeniable truths about laundry:

•Grape juice contains a built-in homing device that is programmed to seek out Mom's "dry clean only" dresses.

•If you want an item to shrink, no amount of scalding water and intense dryer heat will change its molecular structure one bit. However, if it's already a bit snug, it'll shrink while waiting to be washed.

•Red tablecloths are capable of removing themselves from the dining room table, traveling to the laundry room, opening up the washer lid, and diving into a load of your husband's white socks, T-shirts, and underwear. (Your husband will then blame you for all of his pink unmentionables.)

•Some clothes (usually those belonging to a ten-year-old) have a boomerang effect. As soon as you set a pile of clean laundry on the edge of the clothing owner's bed, it will return itself to the dirty laundry pile — with the clothes still folded.

And the pile gets bigger and bigger and bigger.

It's hard to feel significant when it seems all you're doing is folding the same pair of Princess Jasmine pajamas you folded yesterday — and probably the day before that, too.

At times I've even wondered if anyone knows, if anyone even cares, what I do. Does God even care? Mostly, though, I'm usually thinking: *I hate doing laundry.*

Not so with my friend, Polly — and she doesn't even own a dryer. Polly loves doing laundry. She loves watching her sheets hanging on the line and blowing in the breeze.

"You're nuts," I told her one day as I watched her hang diapers.

"Maybe so, "she answered, "but for some reason I feel close to God out here. I know this will sound hokey, but I feel the Lord speaks to me through my laundry. He's like the bleach I use on Jay's socks. They go in the washer dirty, yet come out clean. Hokey, right?"

I laughed at the time, but the more I thought about it, the less hokey it sounded. I realized that Polly's clothesline is, for her, a place of worship…and that she's not nuts.

I have to confess, I've yet to associate the buzzer on my dryer with a call to worship, but I have encountered God a few times over a pile of dirty socks. Perhaps Polly is right that God inhabits the ordinary and commonplace — including stubborn stains. He is not only God in the miraculous, but also God in the mundane.

This I know for sure: He bleaches whiter than snow.

"Let us not become weary in doing good, for at the proper time we will reap a harvest if we do not give up" (Galatians 6:9).

CHAPTER SIX

Get On Board that Potty Train

"WHITE AS SNOW, white as snow...." I began singing a favorite chorus from church as I stood in line. *When I go home...* What was I thinking? I hadn't even left Florida — hadn't even had my complimentary package of roasted peanuts and a beverage — and I was already thinking about going home! Home to the mountain of wet towels, the socks worn in the mud, and the surprise of finding a dryer load of clothes with a red crayon hidden in someone's pocket? No way, José.

I gave Blake's ink stain a spritz of hair spray and dabbed at it with a tissue, then excused myself. I needed to visit the rest room and collect my thoughts. Besides, all good moms know that when one is presented with an opportunity to use the facilities, one must. It's canon law.

My suitcase and I went searching for the ladies' room, or whatever they might call it. You never know these days. A few months ago we were at a Greek restaurant and I had to go. Except, I wasn't sure if I was an Anthron or a Yinekon. In other places I knew I was a Señorita, a Doll, a Doe, and even a stick figure wearing a dress. At the Outback Steakhouse I knew I was a Sheila, rather than a Bloke, but that night at the restaurant…well, it was all Greek to me.

Fortunately, the airport higher-ups had opted for the universal stick figure in a dress. Unfortunately, they made one mistake in the name of technology: auto-flush toilets. Any mom could have told them these things were child-magnets. Every stall was occupied by someone in cartoon-character underpants either giggling as she (or a little he) ran in and out to make the toilets go whoosh or stuffing the end of the toilet paper roll down into the hole to watch it pull in a continuous flush.

Although my children are past such childishness (more or less), I still bore the emotional scars from their earlier preoccupation with public toilets (even before the invention of the auto-flush) and from my preoccupation with them doing their business there. I glanced around the bathroom and totally identified with a mother — on her knees and nearly in tears — trying to coax her little one to "Go for Mommy."

I know from experience: the thing mothers care about most passionately is potty training. The problem is, we're just not content to let things happen naturally. It's as if our children's skill in keeping their Lion King panties dry is a direct indicator of our worth as parents. Not only that, it becomes a contest among mothers. ("All of my babies were trained by their first birthday." "Oh, so late? Mine were all trained by nine months.")

Alison was my first, my guinea pig. I remember setting up her potty chair in the living room, sitting her on it, and keeping her on it until she did something. *Anything.* I tried everything: "I'm a Big Girl" charts with stickers, big girl underwear. (She called it, "big geeeerl undaweeeer.") I even bribed her with M & Ms and wild applause for every tinkle.

I received my own toilet training in the hardware department at Sears. As the story goes, I was a child of even temperament who just happened to have her own timetable (or else I was a rebellious, headstrong little tyke; it all depends on who tells the story). Mom would place me on the toilet at regular intervals (not my regular intervals, mind you) and ask me to do what I preferred doing in my diaper.

The Sears incident took place when I was about three. Still in diapers, I went with my dad to do whatever dads go to do in the hardware department at Sears. And in the middle of us doing it, I had to go. Right then. Right there.

I tugged and I pulled and I yanked my diaper free. Then I pulled my dress up around my waist, marched over to the display toilets, and hopped on the nearest one. My dad, bless his red face, leaped with a single bound over the chuckling crowd and caught me just in time. That is, just in time for me to puddle all over his outstretched arms.

The story has a happy ending. I'm not warped or emotionally disturbed, and at age forty I can use the potty all by myself (and have been doing so for a few years now). But to this day, I have an irrational fear of the bathroom displays at Sears.

Recently I met a woman in Kmart. In her shopping basket was a toy golf club set, a potty chair, and a toddler named Jacob. Although I didn't ask, the woman began talking about IT. "He'll go in the yard. He'll go at the park. He'll go against the car tires. He hits the knot hole on the tree out back, and once he hit — with perfect aim — the entire length of the back fence." She took a breath and continued, "He goes everywhere. He goes around the toilet, but *he won't go in it.* I've tried making a game out of it: 'Aim for the Cheerios in the water, Jacob!' I've tried *everything*." She heaved her shoulders and sighed, obviously at her wits' end. I nodded my head in sympathy. Been there. Done that.

Hearing us talk, a third woman stopped. Her shopping cart was filled with packages of training pants, a potty chair, and a toddler named Erin. "Just last week," she offered, "we were in the ladies' room at a very crowded restaurant. As we walked back to our table, Erin announced, 'Give Mommy a sticker — she went potty all by herself!'"

In a short time, the aisle filled with mothers, toddlers, potty chairs, and potty paraphernalia. As we stood there, passionately discussing the bathroom habits of little ones, the very subjects of our discussion — as if on cue — covered their ears with their hands while ringleader Jacob shouted, "NO MORE POTTY TALK!"

But potty talk is what moms do. How to do it, when to do it. Potty chair or regular toilet? Training pants, big girl underwear, Pull-Up disposables? Do we call it pee-pee or urine? Poo-poo or…what? Do we employ what one parenting magazine called the "Sit-'Em-On-the-Pot Plot" or let the child decide in her own time? What if she's not trained by preschool? What if she's not trained by kindergarten? Will I still be changing her diapers the day of her high school graduation?

When Laura came along, I opted for the *qué será, será* approach. By then I was in my thirties and tired. I'd never heard of a high school graduate in diapers, so I figured she'd either get the hang of it or be in The *Guinness Book of World Records* as the oldest living diaper wearer.

By age two-and-a-half she had reached a point where she could get her own diaper, lay it out on the floor, take off her wet one, climb on the dry one, and pull it up across her bottom.

That's when I decided if you're big enough to change your own diaper, you're probably big enough to use the potty.

Out went *qué será, será.* In came Intensive Potty Training 101. "Laura, you want to wear big girl underwear like Alison, don't you?"

"No."

"Laura, you want to go in the potty for Mommy, don't you?"

"No."

"Laura, you want to go for Daddy, don't you?"

"No."

I changed tactics. "Laura, if you go in the potty, you can flush it bye-bye."

"Don't want to."

I changed tactics again. "Sit on the pot and GO!"

She didn't. She wouldn't. Instead of happy sounds of tinkle echoing through the house, there was weeping and wailing and gnashing of teeth — mine. Meanwhile, Laura happily changed her own diaper and calmly played with her Legos in her room.

After a week or so of unsuccessful training, I reached my limit. In a last-ditch desperate measure, I grabbed my car keys, tucked Laura in her car seat, gave her a boxed apple juice to drink, and went off…to the hardware department at Sears. I figured: *It worked with me. Maybe it'll work with my offspring.*

It didn't.

Laura looked over the display toilets, said she liked the blue one, then asked if we could throw pennies in the mall fountain. No bursts of inspiration. No sudden urges to hop on the pot. *Guinness Book of World Records, here we come,* I thought.

Then one day Laura decided diapers were for babies and she was a big girl. That was that. Hallelujah, Amen.

Hallelujah, Amen! I thought, as the mother on her knees in the airport bathroom stood up and sighed and helped her toddler with her overalls. "We can go potty on the airplane!" she sang with the forced enthusiasm possessed only by the mother of a two-year-old with a timetable of her own.

I shook my head and watched her gather up all her things. Like me and so many other frantic mothers before me, she had missed God's perfect answer to the potty training problem: "There is a time for everything, and a season for every activity under heaven" (Ecclesiastes 3:1).

Even potty training.

"Do not be anxious about anything, but in everything, by prayer and petition, with thanksgiving, present your requests to God. And the peace of God, which transcends all understanding, will guard your hearts and your minds in Christ Jesus" (Philippians 4:6-7).

CHAPTER SEVEN

The Ezekiel 16:44 Woman, *or* Help! I'm Turning Into My Mother!

I FINISHED MY BUSINESS, played around with the auto-flush, then went to wash my hands. I don't know what came over me, but when I lifted my head to look in the mirror, I gasped and spun around.

"Mom!" I cried. "What are you doing here?"

When I spun around, she was gone. Only when I looked back in the mirror did she reappear — in my reflection. I half-expected to hear a voice over the loud speaker announcing: "This morning, a woman went into an airport bathroom and turned into her mother. Film at eleven."

I'd heard about it happening to other women. I just never suspected it would happen to me. But there it was, the green-eyed evidence, telling me from the mirror to stand up straight and stop running in the house with scissors — I might poke someone's eye out.

"How are you, Mom?" I asked.

I'm fine, dear. Now wait thirty minutes before you go swimming and remember to always sit like a lady.

Yep. It was Mom, all right. "What have you been up to, Mom?" I asked.

Oh, you know, a little of this, a little of that. I hope you're not sharing your hairbrush with anyone; you don't want to bring home head lice. And remember, always wear clean underwear in case of an accident. Don't chew your fingernails and swallow them; you'll grow a hand in your stomach. Don't sit to close to the television, either; you'll go blind. And drink all your milk.

I couldn't get over it. My mom: there in the bathroom mirror at the Orlando airport. "I miss having you live nearby, Mom," I told her. "When can you come and visit?"

I don't know, dear, but if you put your arm out the car window, it'll blow off. Also, don't put anything in your ear except your elbow. And speaking of ears, you have two of them and only one mouth, so listen twice as much as you speak. Have you done your chores? Do I look like your slave? Am I speaking Swahili? Don't go outside with wet hair; you'll get pneumonia. Feed a cold, starve a fever. Starve a cold, feed a fever. Turn out the light — do you think your dad works for the electric company?

I shook my head. Mom shook hers, too. "Mom! Are you listening to me?"

Don't you raise your voice, young lady. Now, take the biscuits out

*of the oven BEFORE the smoke alarm goes off. Release the steam from
the pressure cooker BEFORE taking off the lid. Put enough gravy on it
and no one will notice the burnt parts. Chocolate gives you pimples.
Pizza gives you pimples. French fries give you pimples. Wash your face.
Don't wash your face so much — you'll get pimples.*

Blinking in surprise, I remembered a verse I'd read that week:
"Behold, everyone who quotes proverbs will quote this proverb
concerning you, saying 'Like mother, like daughter'" (Ezekiel
16:44 NASB). Like mother, like daughter, indeed.

I peered into the mirror again and shook my head in disbelief.
Not only had my face become hers, but so had my voice. I remembered telling Laura just a few days earlier: "Eat your vegetables; it'll
make your hair curly." Now, I'm a reasonably intelligent person. I
know the eating of vegetables has no scientific correlation to the
curling of hair. But my mother always said it, and it just sort of
slipped out of my mouth, too.

That's not an isolated incident either. I say things like:
"Because I'm your mother, and I said so," "I'll give you something
to cry about!" and "You just wait 'til your father gets home!" Last
week I marched into Alison's bedroom, angry over a sink full of
unwashed dishes, and announced, "I have a bone to pick with
you, young lady." I cringed every time I heard that growing up,
and I cringed as I said it.

It's not just the voice; it's not just the face. It's everything else.
I've acquired "The Looks." There are two. The first Look consists
of pursed lips, narrowed eyes, and flared nostrils, accompanied by
loud, rhythmic breathing. This Look says, "You'd better stop what
you're doing *right now.*" This Look is reserved for horse play in
church, singing the Name Game song ("Martha, Martha, bo
bartha, banana fanna fo fartha...") while trying to make naughty

words, or making a gagging face as your Aunt Sylvia sets a prune-stuffed Cornish hen in front of you at her dinner table.

The second Look is more woeful. It consists of puppy dog eyes, a slight tilt of the head, and a faraway gaze. This Look says, "(Sigh), if you insist on doing_____ (sigh), then you might as well cut my heart out with a knife." This Look works well with hand gestures, such as a slow, rhythmic beating of the breast, a back of the palm to the forehead, or a holding of the head with both hands. This Look is reserved for any number of heartbreaking occasions: the discovery of a spilled glass of milk on the just-cleaned carpeting, a refusal to wear the geeky outfit your mother picked out especially for you, times when she insists that you "go ahead and enjoy yourself and don't think about me" and you do just that, or your announcement at age nineteen that you're leaving home (or you're not leaving home).

Really, I shouldn't have been surprised by this turning into my mother thing. When I turned thirty-six, my mother, aunt, grandmother, and I went out for coffee and pie. There at the restaurant, my grandmother took my hands, patted them, and confided, "I've always liked you in pink, Patricia."

"Thank you, Grandma," I said, "but Patricia's my mother. I'm Nancy."

She pushed her glasses down to the end of her nose and squinted her eyes. "Are you sure, dear?"

I stared into the airport mirror. *No, Grandma, I'm not sure....* I do the very things my mother did that I swore I'd never do. I apologize to bugs before I kill them. I wrap gifts in brown grocery bags, stapled shut with a bow slapped on top. In the event of an emergency, I, too, get down on my knees...and wash the kitchen floor. Mom always said, "In case rescue workers have to come, I don't want them to think we're slobs." That never made sense to me as a child, but (gulp!) now it does.

Although I'm not all that crazy about this metamorphosis from normal human being to a junior version of Mom, I suppose it wouldn't be terrible to be like her. When we were younger, Mom was the Kool-Aid mom on the block. She did cartwheels on the lawn. She let us dig rivers and lakes in the sand box, then flood it with the hose. She made the best apple pie and took us to church each Sunday morning. And I'll never forget my mother in her lavender tutu, dancing to "The Nutcracker Suite" as the Sugar Plum Fairy for the Nevada Avenue Elementary School Christmas play.

Now she lives with my dad on a beach in Mexico, racing her dune buggy and four-wheeled motorcycle up and down the sand, fishing and painting desert scenes on whatever flat surface she can find. Her hair isn't platinum anymore, and she hung up her toe shoes and tutu a long time ago. I miss her, but she's always with me. I have her nose. I have her cheeks. I have her, *If you swallow your gum, your stomach will explode,* and her, *You'll thank me someday.* I have her heart.

It's one of those undeniable, indisputable laws of the universe, this turning into your mother thing, and it's happening to my daughters, too. Just the other day I noticed Alison had my cheekbones. The older she gets, the less she looks like Barry and the more she looks like me.

It's not just physical characteristics, either. Both girls are taking on my internal traits. Alison has my nervous stomach when things get stressful. She also has my need for solitude and my love for simple pleasures. I hope she'll one day have my confidence that God "is able to do immeasurably more than all we ask or imagine, according to his power that is at work within us" (Ephesians 3:20).

When I think of Laura, I see myself back in middle school doing the same things she does now: passing notes, cracking jokes, irritating teachers with her constant chatter. Laura has my sense of fun and my love for the limelight. My hope for her is that she'll take on my awe of a holy, righteous God, and that her desire to do what's right will be stronger than her desire to do what's fun for the moment.

I look into the mirror and see my mother, but I also see my daughters. That's the way it works. Mother molds daughter who molds granddaughters.

There in the bathroom, I peered into the mirror again. This time I was gazing into my daughters' faces. "Girls," I said, "like it or not, this is your future. The crooked nose, the turkey drumstick legs, and yes...even the off-key renditions of 'Starlight Express.'"

As I picked up my suitcase to leave the bathroom, I took a final look. "Just remember," I said. "I don't want you to look like me. I want you to look like Jesus."

"Be imitators of me, as I am of Christ" (1 Corinthians 11:1 RSV).

CHAPTER EIGHT

Carry Me, Carry You, Carry On

I WALKED OUT of the bathroom with a familiar pain in my side. (It was either gas or guilt.) Thinking about the girls had caused a twinge of doubt, and it was twinging itself right under my left rib cage. I dragged my suitcase over to a bench to collect my thoughts and wait for the pain to subside.

It wasn't as if I were leaving them forever. I planned on return-ing...eventually. I just needed a break. I also needed an antacid, so I started rummaging through my purse for one.

Just then an ear-splitting wail vibrated through the airport as a two-foot-high mass of brown curls in blue overalls threw back her head and screamed, "Carry me, Mommy!"

Mommy already had a suitcase in one hand, a duffel bag in the other, her purse slung around her neck, and airline tickets between her teeth as she sprinted down the corridor. The Wailer followed close behind, stopping every few inches to scream and demand to be carried.

I knew what was going to happen, and sure enough...it did. After about the fifth wail, Mommy put down her suitcase, bent over, lifted her daughter onto her hip, picked her suitcase back up, then resumed her mad dash to wherever she was headed, barely missing a step. The wailing ceased, and all was well with the little girl. Mommy, however, would walk lop-sided the rest of her life....

One of the most amazing things about motherhood is the ability of a woman's body to do seventy-three things at once while a child is carried on the hip. It helps that God designed our lower half to protrude into the next time zone. And while it doesn't look all that appealing in a bathing suit, it serves as a dandy baby saddle.

I knew a woman who wallpapered her entire dining room while carrying a baby on her hip. Not only that, she'd walk around the house while holding her son, a laundry basket, a caddy for all her household cleaning products, and a mop. Not only would she carry them all, she could fold her laundry and clean her house without setting anything down. She cooked dinner, played Mah Jong, did step aerobics, cultivated a compost heap, and sanded her garage door...all while attached to that baby. People would travel for miles just to see this amazing woman in action.

She had just one problem. Whenever she put her son down for a nap, she could walk only in circles.

Carry me, Mommy! Although it had been ages since I'd heard those words, I still felt their impact. They meant, "Mommy, drop whatever you're doing. I'm more important! I'm more urgent! Make room for me, Mommy!"

Carry me, Mommy! Only, in my family it's more like: "Will you drive me and Kelly and Melanie (and the rest of the seventh grade) to the mall?" or "I know you're busy, but will you watch my cheerleading routine (for the twelve millionth time)?" Thankfully, the days of kids (physically) riding sidesaddle are over (too bad the "saddle" still remains).

As my gas/guilt pain returned, I continued to fish through my purse for an antacid. However, since I'd accumulated so much junk over the years, I couldn't find anything. It weighed a ton and dug grooves into my shoulder when I carried it. That's when I decided, as much as I needed to do something about the pain in my side, what I really needed was to clean out the catch-all I called my purse.

As I dumped its contents onto the bench (and chased the button I'd intended to sew back on Alison's tapestry vest) I realized a person could read my whole life from that pile of stuff.

A ticket stub from *Pocahontas*? She's a sucker for Mel Gibson, even if it is just his voice. A pair of sunglasses with one lens fallen out? Just call her "Squinty." Three rolls of breath mints? Don't believe her when she says she sucks on them to keep her throat moist — she's terrified of being caught with bad breath.

A wallet full of expired coupons? This is a shopper who, once she gets to the checkout counter, is too preoccupied to conduct her business in an economical manner because her child is either begging for a pack of Skittles ("Mom, have I told you lately that I love you?") or has chosen that exact moment to explain the romance between somebody named Plaid Boy and somebody else named Tiffany P.

My Webster's pocket dictionary revealed either a woman with a thirst for knowledge or one who needs a four-inch book to keep her glove compartment from rattling. A pile of unmailed bills showed a woman who's about to get past-due notices in the mail. A dozen black ink pens showed that this purse belonged to a writer, or a pen hoarder — or maybe both.

I threw out the wads of ATM receipts, the three-year-old lay-away tickets from items long outgrown or broken, the to-do lists with items left undone, a doodled-on church bulletin, and a recipe for a spice cake made with pureed pickled beets that I had thought sounded so disgusting it was probably delicious. (I never found out. The recipe stayed in my purse, collecting pen scribbles, for over two years.)

Out went the fuzzy, broken, cherry-flavored Chapstick, the piece of paper with "HERITAGE PROPANE, call G. at 2 and del by ?" scrawled on one side and "Monkey Ward/belt for tred" on the other. Out went the grape stems and Snickers wrapper and seven proofs of purchase from the bags of weed and feed treatment (for a contest that expired the previous month).

In days past, my purse housed such things as plastic baggies of Cheerios to pacify a cranky toddler, leaky Tommy Tippee cups (for same toddler), wads of ABC ("already been chewed") gum, extra diapers, bottles of baby Tylenol, and fuzzy Binkies (pacifiers, to the uninitiated).

As a mother, my purse has been a catchall for Sunday school take-home papers, Barbie dolls confiscated at a restaurant dinner table after Barbie (against warnings from me) ended up in the mashed potatoes, wet socks, half-eaten Happy Meals, and half-broken Happy Meal toys. It's been sat on and drooled on, and it rarely has money in it.

It's been forever since I purchased a purse solely on its appearance. "Does it go with this outfit?" was replaced long ago by "Will it hold a Cabbage Patch doll, a box of graham crackers, a roll of paper towels, and an Etch-a-Sketch?" The family refers to my current purse as "Mom's cow." They insist I went into the store and asked the saleslady for a side of beef with a shoulder strap and lots of pockets. They laugh…until they want me to carry something for them.

But that's what a mom does. She carries her children's burdens as best she can, enabling them to walk unencumbered through life. It's when she fails to give her children over to God that she becomes stoop-shouldered from the weight of her load.

I rubbed my sore shoulder. *Oh, Lord,* I prayed, *I have so many doubts and fears concerning the girls. Alison can't decide on a career…she's lonely…her friends have all gone away to college and she's left at home…she can't see her life ever changing….*

And Laura…am I doing the right things with her? She's twelve years old and she's never done a load of laundry! She has a hard time in math. She worries herself sick before a softball game. Her feet won't stop growing….

I rubbed my shoulder again. *Father, show me the things I can do to help them and the things they need to do for themselves. The rest, Lord, I give over to You.*

As I finished sorting through everything, I finally found the roll of antacid I'd been looking for and popped one in my mouth. Then, having discarded those things that had encumbered me, I stood and marveled at the wonderful feeling that came with dropping all that unnecessary weight.

And my purse wasn't heavy anymore, either.

"Praise be to the Lord, to God our Savior, who daily bears our burdens" (Psalm 68:19).

CHAPTER NINE

Forgive Me, Kodak, for I Have Sinned

I STILL HADN'T DECIDED where I wanted to go, so I sat back down on the bench. As I did, a woman tapped me on the shoulder.

"Mind if I sit here?" she asked.

I patted the space next to me. "Go right ahead."

She flopped down and repinned the bun in her hair, then removed the camera around her neck. "Would you mind taking a picture of me?"

Before I could answer, she handed me her camera and with a huge grin said, *"Fromage!"*

I snapped the picture and gave back her camera.

"Thanks," she said. "I'm meeting my son, Markie. He's coming in from Atlanta. Visiting the grandparents for an early Thanksgiving." She put her camera back around her neck. "I'll call this series, 'Waiting For Markie.'" She opened a satchel the size of Rhode Island, pulled out a photo album marked: Volume IX,

SEPT — OCT, and began turning the pages.

"That's Markie on his first day of third grade this year." She pointed to the photo with the caption: "Third Grade or Bust!" The following pages showed Markie in various poses of getting on and off the school bus, Markie holding up his notebook and Power Rangers lunch box, Markie tying his shoes, Markie scratching his nose. Each photo was evenly spaced and symmetrically precise, each one individually captioned. ("Oh, look! Markie empties the trash!" "Markie's tuna sandwich is yum, yum, yummy!")

With the last photo of Markie removing the seeds from a pumpkin ("Look at that Markie scoop!"), Markie's mom put her Volume IX back in her bag and sighed.

"You must think I'm dreadful showing you such old pictures, but you know how it is. I just haven't gotten around to categorizing this week's batch." She lowered her voice. "I haven't even taken in yesterday's film yet. Isn't that terrible of me?"

Finally, I got a chance to speak. "That's not terrible at all! I know exactly how it is. Don't beat yourself up. I've done the same thing myself."

She smiled and looked me over. I squirmed in my seat and prayed she wouldn't ask me The Question.

Too late. "You have kids, right?" she asked. "Can I see your pictures?"

I fished through my wallet and handed over my most recent pictures of the girls.

"Oh." She handed them back to me. "They're pretty. Are they walking yet?"

I squirmed again and gulped. "Yes, they're both walking," I said. "See the one with the brown curls and brown eyes? That's Alison. She's nineteen. And the one sitting in the turkey roaster, licking a popsicle? That's Laura. She's twelve now."

The woman clicked her tongue and patted my shoulder. It was a pity pat.

Forgive me, Kodak, for I have sinned. I am what you call photographically challenged and the *only* mother in North America (or at least in my circle of friends) who does not own a (working) camera or a camcorder.

I wasn't always camera impaired. In fact, I once considered myself the Ansel Adams of Florida's Nature Coast. With my trusty pocket Instamatic and the fastest shutter finger this side of the Mississippi, I'd artistically pose my daughters in varying degrees of leaning, stooping, head tilting, and mid-air flight. By age three, each girl could say "cheese" in several different languages. I became one of those obnoxious parents who, in the middle of the preschool "I Am a Carrot" play, shouts: "Smile, baby! Wave to Mommy!" and flashes until everyone in the room is seeing stars and/or muttering, "Get that woman out of here!"

Actually, taking the pictures isn't my biggest problem. Getting the film developed is my downfall. I'm embarrassed to admit this, but I have rolls of film dating back to our 1985 trip to Idaho still in the kitchen junk drawer. When other moms whip out their stack of prints from the previous day's tire rotation, I whip out a roll of film.

"See this?" I say. "Picture Alison, only shorter and with braces, and Laura in a stroller in front of the sign at Sea World."

Once (and only once) I attempted a family group shot. I borrowed a friend's tripod and 35 mm with a timer and set them up in the living room. Then, aiming off-center at a cat's paw print on the wall, I strategically arranged my family on the couch and told them to think happy thoughts.

"Look natural," I ordered. "Smile, but don't show too much teeth. Fix your hair. Don't look at the camera. And pretend you like each other." I gave instructions for ten minutes straight as we waited for the flash. By the time the camera finally went off, Alison had puffed out her cheeks in boredom, Laura had started yawning, and Barry had lost his patience altogether.

The photo came out showing Alison looking like a blowfish, Laura with her mouth wide open in an apparent attempt to catch flies, Barry wearing a "Get this over with, will ya, huh?" expression, and me sitting beside them...grinning the grin of idiots and fools. The only thing in focus was the cat's paw print. That's when I decided to leave photography to the experts and rely on the kindness of friends to supply me with three-by-five glossies of my children.

Fortunately, there are plenty of parents who know how to take pictures without disrupting the entire school assembly, who remember to remove their lens caps, and who get their film developed in the same decade in which their photos were taken.

That means, whenever Laura is up on stage lip-synching "Oh, Shenandoah" along with twenty other kids in the seventh grade chorus, I can count on at least a dozen parents to have a print of my child (her hair falling in her face and her mouth twisted in an awkward scowl) that they are more than willing to give me. Likewise, when Alison goes anywhere with her friend Tracie and Tracie's mother (who takes pictures of the girls' every sneeze), I'm assured of at least a half dozen shots of Alison in varying stages of opening her mouth.

Despite my Just Say No resolve to leave the shutter clicking to others, I did give in last year at Alison's graduation. I managed to take her picture without disrupting the ceremony and take the film to get developed *and* pick it up. But I've yet to send pictures to the relatives or replace the picture in my wallet (of her in her high chair) with her senior photo…or even her sixth grade school picture with her eyes shut tight.

I sighed as I put the girls' photos back in my wallet. By that time, Markie's mom had picked up her things.

"I don't know what I'd do if I didn't have my photos," she said a bit self-righteously, then excused herself and moved on.

A pang of guilt started to edge its way into my thinking, but I immediately chased it away. Just because I've been banned from yelling, "Say cheese!" and I don't have an up-to-date, chronologically arranged, alphabetized, and cleverly-captioned photo album of my children, that doesn't mean I don't have a full-color record of their every stage and rite of passage hidden in my heart.

Etched in my memory is a brown-eyed cherub named Alison in a pale blue dress, up to her elbows in chocolate cake on her first birthday. I see her at age two, riding her red tricycle around the living room of our Portland, Maine, apartment and chasing a red plastic ball down the frozen beach, wearing her "Libby's, Libby's, Libby's" snow hat. When she was three, she took her first airplane trip to California and had to sit on top of a suitcase in order to watch the in-flight movie.

I can't ever forget my first glimpse of Laura. With her pug nose, swollen-shut eyes, and chubby pink cheeks, my immediate thought was: "How could I have given birth to a pig?" She ate her first bug at eighteen months and let the neighbor boy drag her around the apartment's greasy carport in her white sunsuit when she was three. On the Christmas Eve of her fourth year, she sang "Away In a Manger" dressed as an angel in white, a silver garland in her straight brown hair — and black high-top sneakers on her feet.

The photo in my memory of Alison at age nine is that of a moonfaced girl with a mane of dark hair, carefully picking out "Clementine" on the piano. At age ten, the year she didn't eat, the picture changes to a gray-skinned, sunken-eyed girl reading alone in her room. Laura at age nine is up in the air, red and white pom-poms in her hands, and at age eleven is at home plate, popping a fly ball over the second baseman's head, or dipping slices of pepperoni in chocolate pudding at Wendy's — then eating them!

I can't forget Alison's first day of high school, first driving lesson, first time driving alone, first job, first car, or how she looked in her black cap and gown, walking onto the stage to get her high school diploma.

I have a box stuffed with photos in the hall closet. Some of their edges are wrinkled, many of them are out of focus and discolored or faded. Most of them are not what you would consider artistic masterpieces or even aesthetically pleasing. We're not a photogenic family.

When Markie's mom pulled out her photo album, I thought for a moment about getting a new camera for Christmas or at least getting the film developed from years past. But then the urge passed. I remembered that photos too often record our awkward posturing and outward imperfections. They fail to reflect the beauty within and the pain and struggles that make us look more like God.

Those are the images I want captured.

Those are the pictures I carry with me.

"I thank my God upon every remembrance of you" (Philippians 1:3 KJV).

CHAPTER TEN

Move Over, Ward Cleaver, Make Room for Mr. New Dad

RATS! I THOUGHT. *I can't start getting sentimental now, not right in the middle of running away!* I tried pushing away my thoughts of the girls by concentrating on the people walking through the airport: a man in plaid golf pants, his female companion in a green jogging suit, a dark-haired man with long sideburns and a white jumpsuit, snarling his lip and shaking his hip.

Things were going fine until I noticed a young man who didn't look that much older than Alison. He was dressed in a dark gray suit with shiny black shoes and slicked back brown hair, but the diaper bag flung over his shoulder looked out of place with his business ensemble. As I watched him juggle a cell phone and a baby bottle (plus the baby attached to the bottle), my thoughts turned to

Barry, and once again I was awash in sentimentality.

What can I say about a man who served chicken drumsticks at Mrs. Chandler's first-grade class Thanksgiving feast and who once dressed up in air force jungle fatigues and a batting helmet for children's church, while carrying a metal trash can lid to serve as a visual aid to illustrate the armor of God? Or who does the "reindeer dance" on request (a high-stepping, sort of running in place, done while singing, "De-de-de-de, de-de-de")? Or who, despite being outnumbered in a household of six females (three human, three feline), keeps his sense of humor in the middle of, as he calls it, "all that girl stuff"?

He wanted a son. Charles Thomas Kennedy. A son. Someone with whom he could share manly, macho guy things like baseball and football and going wee-wee in the woods while on manly, macho camping trips.

He wanted someone with whom he could have arm hair pulling contests. Once he attempted it with me, but as hard as I tried, I just couldn't bring myself to grab onto his arm hair and yank it until it either ripped out by the roots or he cried, "Uncle!" (the rules of the game). Not only that, he (thankfully) couldn't do anything to hurt me, which whittled his pool of partners in barbarianism down to none. He settled for "noogie" contests with me...but he wanted a son.

I'll never forget the night the three of us (Barry, me, and my pregnant stomach) went to the movies. The Bad News Bears was playing, and Barry wanted the vicarious experience of coaching his son's Little League team. He said he chose that movie for its critical acclaim and well-crafted script, but I knew better. I had seen him stash his baseball mitt in the back seat of our car. (For what, I wasn't sure. It had to have been a guy thing.)

The movie was about a little girl (Tatum O'Neal) with a killer pitching arm and her relationship with her bum of a Little League coach (Walter Matthau). Not to Barry, however. Every boy on that screen was his son (my stomach). He didn't say it out loud, but every time a boy caught an outfield fly or hit a line drive up the middle, his face said, "That's my boy." Then he'd reach over, pat my stomach, and puff his chest with pride.

Then the wimpy boy came onto the field.

He'd been on the bench all season. Nobody liked him, not even the audience. He whined, slobbered his food, and never wiped his nose.

The game — THE Game (a championship or something) — was at whatever the final make-it-or-break-it moment is in a ball game. The batter hit a fly ball that headed directly toward the wimpy blond-haired kid in baggy pants. There was no way this kid was going to catch this ball. No way.

But Barry prayed. I saw his lips move. "Please God, let him catch it." As he prayed, he squeezed his box of Jujubes in one hand and my hand in the other.

As the miracle happened and the wimpy kid caught the ball, I witnessed, for the first time, my husband cry. Tears welled in his eyes. "My son," he said. "That's my son."

He wanted a son, yet when the doctor said, "It's a girl," there was never a happier man in all of the western hemisphere. He picked himself up off the floor and vowed to all of heaven and earth that he would be the best New Dad he could be.

He began the next evening during hospital visiting hours. Someone had seen him drive up, so I fluffed my pillows, brushed my hair, and waited for Mr. New Dad to visit me and our new daughter. I waited. And waited. And waited. Finally, after half an hour had gone by, I plodded out into the hall and discovered that my husband — who had witnessed the birth of his daughter face down on the delivery room floor — had gone from, "I don' know nothin' about birthin' no babies," to being Mr. Labor and Delivery Man as he shared his previous night's labor experience with a strange woman in labor on a gurney. I laughed as he told her in all sincerity: "I know just how you feel."

Barry is a wonderful man, but he don' know nothin' about birthin' no babies. He thinks he understands women, and I let him think he does. But the truth is: he don'. During my entire pregnancy, I cried every morning on our way to work. We'd leave our apartment and drive the fourteen miles to the air force base with me sobbing the whole time. By the time we arrived, I'd blow my nose, take a breath, and be fine.

Now, Barry didn't understand this. And because he didn't, we'd have the same conversation every morning.

Him: "Why are you crying?"

Me: "I don't know. I just am."

Him: "Is it something I said? Is it something I did? Should I call the doctor?"

Me: "I'm fine. I'm. Just. Crying."

Every morning the same conversation. Barry said he understood, but Barry didn't understand. I understood when he cried at *The Bad News Bears*, but he's yet to understand a woman's hormonally-induced tears. And God gave him daughters to further confuse him.

When Alison reached the preteen, hormones-from-hell, temper-tantrum stage all girls go through and started flinging herself against a wall or flailing herself on the floor in convulsive sobs because we ran out of peanut butter or something of that nature, Barry could only look on in utter bewilderment.

He'd ask me, "Why is she crying?"

I'd answer, "I don't know. She just is."

Then he'd ask, "Is it something I said? Is it something I did? Should I call the doctor?"

I'd tell him, "She's fine. She's. Just. Crying."

One day, in all earnestness, he asked me if she needed psychological help and offered to take a second job to pay for it. Finally, I sat him down and explained to him, "There's nothing wrong with her. She's just a girl."

He said he understood, but....

Over the years, Mr. New Dad adapted quite well to his role. He became proficient being out of the house at diaper-changing time and adept at not hearing a baby's cry at 3:00 A.M. However, their rare nocturnal silences woke him up regularly. He'd shoot up in bed, cock his ear toward the hallway, and shake me awake.

"What's that?" he'd ask.

"What? I don't hear anything. Go back to sleep," I'd say.

A few minutes later he'd spring up again, sit in the dark, and listen. Then, when I had been fully roused out of my precious sleep, he would crawl out of bed and pad down the hall to check on the baby. She'd be sound asleep, and he'd put his hand on her back to feel her breathe. Still not convinced, he'd put a mirror under her nose to catch steam. Then, when she'd wake up crying, he'd go back to bed and let me do, as he called it, "the mommy thing."

I continued to watch the man in the airport doing "the daddy thing" with his new baby. By then he'd put the bottle back in the diaper bag, draped a cloth over his left shoulder, and put the baby on his right shoulder (which meant he ended up with baby spit-up all down his right side). I couldn't help laughing. He reminded me so much of Barry and newborn Alison.

Alison arrived in the middle of football season, and on her first Sunday afternoon home from the hospital, Barry decided it was time to initiate his daughter into the fellowship of armchair quarterbacks. I'd gone to the store, leaving him alone with his six-pound, thirteen-ounce, future Baltimore Colts fan — his future Baltimore Colts fan with a wet diaper, that is.

Now Barry believes in roomy comfort: in clothes, in furniture...in diapers. He expertly set his future Baltimore Colts fan down on her open Pamper, brought up the front as he had practiced on our stuffed Curious George monkey, and taped the thing shut (leaving ample leg "breathing" room). Then he went back into the living room, propped his future Baltimore Colts fan on his lap, and within minutes, felt something warm and wet on his pants.

Another diaper; another loose, roomy fit; another puddle in the lap. This went on all afternoon. By the time I arrived home, Barry, still damp from his baptism into parenthood, met me at the door with outstretched arms and wet diapers scattered all over. Thoroughly frustrated, he wailed: "Grab the manual and see what it says about leaks!"

Eventually, he caught on. He grew to realize that little girls are not little boys. He learned that they actually like wearing frilly dresses and patent leather shoes and drinking tea with a group of stuffed animals as their guests. And he learned girls sometimes cry just because.

They (whoever "they" are) say a girl grows up to marry a man just like her dad. (I know I did.) In Barry's case, his daughters would do well to find such a man who is dependable and strong, responsible and caring, with a sacrificial love and a heart for helping people in need.

As a dad, Barry is far from perfect. He is, however, the dad God decided Alison and Laura needed.

In her early teen years, Alison locked horns regularly with Barry. After a heated battle, she'd run to her room vowing never to marry a man like him. Ironically, a few months ago as she and a friend discussed all the things they wanted in a husband, Alison discovered — much to her surprise and Barry's chagrin — that the things she wanted most (among other characteristics: responsible, hard-working, good sense of humor, strong, easy-going, good with his hands, handy around the house, and sports-minded) described her dad.

What kind of a dad is he to the girls? One who tries his hardest to do what's right. And although he, as an earthly father, sometimes falls short, I pray that my daughters will know they have a heavenly Father who has promised to fill every void. When they do find husbands, my only hope is that they find men who are committed to loving their wives (my daughters!), serving Jesus...and applying their children's diapers a little on the snug side!

"He will turn the hearts of the fathers to their children, and the hearts of the children to their fathers" (Malachi 4:6).

"Let Go! —
No, Don't!"
Cha-Cha-Cha

GRIPPED BY A WAVE of nostalgic sentimentality, I toyed with the idea
of turning around and going home. I'd lost much of the steam that
fueled my initial escape, and I wasn't sure if I had any left to continue. Still…I hadn't had my adventure. I hadn't found that
glorious rest I needed so badly. I hadn't even been gone long
enough for the family to notice!

Another wave of sentimentality washed over me: Laura sleeping with her teddy bear "Bob." Alison and her sweet notes to me.
Barry and those arm muscles of his.…

I tried putting my head between my knees, hoping the
rolling waves were like nausea and would go away in time. From
that position I chanted, "Remember the mustard. Remember the
mustard.…"

Remember the whining and the groaning and the spilled raspberry Slurpees in the car. Remember the place mats used to wipe

up soda spills and the hair-spray residue on every flat surface in the house. Remember the dog eating cold chili out of the pot while the girls use the blow dryer on him after a bath.

I lifted my head and tried growling, but my *grr* came out more like a *guh-guh-guh.* "Remember the mustard. *Guh-guh-guh.*"

And the footprints on the wall.... *Guh-guh-guh.* The rainy-day indoor soccer games, the washable markers soaking in a tub of sudsy water, and the For School Lunches Only packs of cookies purchased on Friday, eaten up by Sunday night. *Guh-guh-guh.*

By that last *guh,* I noticed most of the people around me had backed away. The only one left was an elderly woman walking by. She fumbled in her purse and, handing me a tissue, said, "Here. Blow your nose, honey."

As hard as I tried, I just couldn't gather up enough of whatever it takes to let out the kind of real, Tony-the-Tiger-type growl I'd given earlier. So I blew my nose, picked up my suitcase, and left to go back home.

By then my suitcase had doubled in size and tripled in weight. I pushed it through the airport terminal, looking for the exit. I pushed. I stopped. I pushed some more. I bumped into a dozen people, all (it seemed) straight out of Norman Rockwell paintings. Mothers in straight skirts, white blouses with Peter Pan collars, and sensible shoes stood holding onto fresh-scrubbed, servicemen sons home on leave from Over There. Clear-skinned young women in page boy flips and plastic headbands waving good-bye to gray-suited young men in red ties and wing-tipped shoes. Bosomy grandmas and twinkly-eyed grandpas clutching wiggly grandchildren for one last hug before their departure on Flight 547 to Milwaukee.

For a brief moment, I imagined a similar Rockwellesque

scene greeting me at home: the girls skipping out to meet me (a "Hello, Mommy Dearest," on their lips and two shiny apples in their hands for their beloved mother) and Barry greeting me with a single red rose between his teeth and a glint in his dark brown eyes.

My thoughts were interrupted by an ear-splitting, "Let go — give it to me!" as two messy-haired young girls in torn jeans — one wearing a Nine Inch Nails T-shirt and the other with a nose ring — played tug of war with a black leather jacket.

"Mom!" Nose Ring called to a harried-looking woman carrying a suitcase under each arm and a shoulder bag in her teeth. "She won't let go! Make her gimme my jacket!"

Suddenly I felt confused. Not only couldn't I find the exit, I didn't know whether to continue my runaway adventure. I looked around for a sign, remembering that sometimes God sends supernatural messages to His children. All I found was a shoeshine stand and a poster urging me to visit Disney World during my visit to Orlando.

Then I saw my sign.

It said: "EXIT."

I approached the double glass doors and, as if by magic (or technology), they opened wide. I shoved my suitcase through them and huffed and puffed my way to my car on Level....

I forgot.

I wandered around Level One, trying to remember where I parked. As I lugged my suitcase around the garage, I overheard a woman who was half-sobbing, half-laughing (a phenomenon known only to mothers).

"Oh, Justin!" she kept repeating. "Oh, Justin!"

It appeared that Justin (about age three) had gotten into a box of chocolates, and — as in life — didn't quite know what he'd get. However, his mother knew, albeit too late. Justin had gotten a mess. Not only had he smeared the chocolates all over his face and hands, he'd managed to embed them into his blond hair, in his ears, and all over his gray sweat suit. It also looked like there was melted chocolate all over his car seat, the back of the driver's seat, and the rear bumper of the car. Next, Justin was headed for his mother's yellow skirt.

"Let go, Justin!" she cried as he grabbed her hem and buried his face in the folds of the material.

I chuckled to myself and sighed, relieved that I was past the chocolatey-face-on-my-clothes stage. Then I emitted a laugh/cry of my own as I reminded myself: *You may be past gooey hands, but you're not past preteen hormones and requests for shoulder tattoos.* As the late Gilda Radner said, "It's always something."

After several laps I realized my car wasn't on Level One, so I trudged up to Level Two. There, another half-laugh/half-sob caught my attention. It was another mother with another Justin. Only this one was named Caitlin, and she was the one screaming, "Let go!" as she struggled to escape her mother's hand and resume pouncing in puddles of rain water.

Let go! How many times have I heard that? I wondered.

"Let go — I do it myself!"

"Let go, Mom — I can ride my bike myself now."

"Mom, watch me dive off the high dive."

"I'll be home by eleven, Mom. Don't wait up."

Let go! How many times have I said it? First to the drooling infant at my shoulder grabbing a fistful of my hair, then to the Amazing Velcro Toddler stuck to my leg. Next, it was to the obstinate child, determined to hold onto one of her sister's beloved

possessions, then to the too-eager teenager holding onto the
steering wheel of my car and pleading for me to let her drive.

Let go!

It's a precarious dance, this letting go, with parent and child
alternately moving away and clutching tight, both shouting, "Let
go — no, don't!" When the dance is over, the child ultimately ends
up partnered with God, and the parent is left watching from the
sidelines. But until then, the parent-child dance continues, with
each partner occasionally suffering as their toes get stepped on.

I remember teaching Alison to drive. Our dance went something like this: Alison would take two steps forward, dangling my
car keys, waving her learner's permit, and begging, "Come on,
Mom. Let me drive!"

I'd respond by taking two steps backward and listing all the
reasons why she couldn't. ("It's too hot/too cold. There's too much
traffic/not enough traffic. The sun's too high/the moon's too bright.
Wait until after the vernal equinox.")

It's not just that I didn't want her driving — although I *didn't*
want her driving. However, I was acutely aware that when you're
almost seventeen, having your mommy drive you everywhere is a
certain social hazard (akin to having your mommy walk you to the
bus stop — in her bathrobe).

I've been told there's nothing worse than being in a car with
your mother and having her drive up to a red light, stop next to
the "majorly cute" guy in your algebra class, and say loudly (with
the window rolled down), "You're right; he *is* cute!" then call to
him, "Yoo-hoo! Wanna drag?"

Sixteen-year-old daughters tend not to appreciate such social
commentary. Neither do they appreciate a mother's lack of trust in
their driving skills. Once, I hinted that Alison shouldn't drive

because the weatherman had predicted a ten percent chance of rain.

"Mom," she pointed out, "my driver's ed teacher — a paid professional — trusted me to drive on a major highway. *In a downpour.*" She further accused me of thinking that at the first raindrop she'd throw the car into reverse, flip the hood up, and recline the seat back while trying to find the windshield wipers. (It could happen.)

Like I said, it's a precarious dance. Two steps forward ("Mom, let me drive to the store!"). Two steps back ("How about I let you drive to the corner at five miles per hour with lights and emergency flashers on, and I drive back?").

"Mom, you have to let go of me sometime!" Alison cried one day. "Every other teenager in America can drive. I'm an honor student. I know the red light means stop, green light means go, and yellow means 'floor it!'"

So her father and I let go. Let go as she drives, dates, goes off to college, and makes decisions on her own. Let go of Laura, too, as she goes three states away to camp or attends a first school dance. Let go, even as they shout, "I changed my mind — don't let go! I want to be a child forever!"

The dance continues, I thought as I circled Level Three looking for my car. *And the steps keep getting more complicated and more difficult.*

Just then, the roar of a plane passing overhead startled me, and I remembered Laura once asking me, "Is God bigger than the sky?"

"Oh, yes," I assured her at the time. "He's *way* bigger."

Big enough to give us freedom to make our own choices — to let us go — yet to still hold on strong.

"For you were called to freedom, brethren; only do not turn your freedom into an opportunity for the flesh, but through love serve one another" (Galatians 5:13 NASB).

CHAPTER TWELVE

Sense and Momsense

GOD'S GRASP MAY *be strong, but mine certainly isn't,* I thought as I rubbed my sore palms together and continued dragging my suitcase down to Level Two for one more look. Finally, hot and sweaty, I spied my little red Tempo and fumbled through my purse for my keys.

I fumbled through my....

I fumbled....

I peered in through my car window, then made a mental note: *Next time I run away, remember to take the keys out of the ignition before locking the doors.*

Barry always says, give me a week in a new town and I'll learn the names of every tow truck driver, locksmith, and paramedic before Friday. What can I say? It's a gift.

Take the time I was coloring my hair (OK, *one* of the times). I had put the goopy stuff on my head and wrapped it in a plastic grocery bag. While waiting for the required twenty minutes to pass, I remembered that there was a magazine in the car that I wanted to read. So I opened the front door and — as is my unconscious habit — relocked it, stepped outside, and closed the door.

Fortunately, I had the good sense to have a spare key made after an earlier locked-out-of-the-house episode involving a pot of burning pinto beans and two red-eyed, anxious kitties who were left with the smoke alarm blaring while I waited for Larry the Locksmith to come to their (and my) rescue.

Unfortunately, the spare key was hanging on a peg in the laundry room.

Panicked, I ran to my neighbor's — plastic bag, goop, and all — and called Locksmith Larry, who came to my aid forty-five minutes later. I ended up having to rinse the goop out of my hair with the garden hose, and we all lived happily ever after with our Toasted Almond Light Golden Brown #12 patch of grass.

Happily ever after until now, I thought as I studied my situation: one hot, sweaty woman with a sore elbow resulting from pulling a twelve-ton suitcase up and down three levels of the parking garage, a tension headache, and her only set of keys in the ignition of her car.

And a dilemma.

The keys in the car, that wasn't a problem. In fact, that was almost second nature to me. Calling the locksmith...even that wasn't a big deal. Calling from a pay phone...*that* was the problem. Especially when I didn't have any change on me and I had to use my calling card.

I know, I know. A forty-year-old woman should know how to use a pay phone. In theory, I do. In practice.... Well, let's just say that in my case, practice doesn't make perfect.

Telephones are complicated these days. I don't even try to understand deregulation and the break up of Ma Bell; I'm still trying to figure out how to use an AT&T card on a Sprint phone. For some reason I have a mental block, and I've yet to use my phone card properly.

Once, while at a conference, I attempted to call home using my phone card. I followed the instructions both on the phone and on my card. I got a connection and heard the phone ring, but the voice that answered, "Ah-lo! Ah-lo!" didn't belong to anyone in my household.

Oh my, I've called France! I thought. I apologized to the Ah-lo person and hung up the phone. It had always been a phobia of mine that one day I'd call someplace far away like Hong Kong or Russia. Sure enough, I just knew I'd called France. I called the operator right back, and she assured me it was impossible to accidentally call France from a pay phone following the directions on my phone card.

She was right. When I got the bill at the end of the month, it showed I hadn't called France after all.

For $7.95 I'd called Turkey. Ah-lo! Ah-lo!

My telephone troubles at the airport got me thinking about my telephone troubles at home. I mean, why is it kids cannot carry on a telephone conversation while in an upright position? Why must the feet be on a chair and the body on the floor? Or the body on the couch and the head dangling off the side? Why must the cord be stretched to its maximum length (or beyond), or wrapped around a dining room chair, dog, or pair of shoes left in the middle of the floor? And why must the conversations (consisting of nothing more than a series of "I'm sure," "No way," "Like, how?" "Yeah, right," and "Says who?") last for hours? I mean, how long does it take to say, "I'm sure; no way; like, how; yeah, right;" and "says who"?

Guh-guh-grr. I began to growl as I thought about the phone ringing at precisely 3:04 every afternoon (Laura gets home at about 3:03) and continuing until 10:00 P.M. (my bedtime and the time I shut the ringer off), when suddenly I smelled something.

As sweaty as I was in my sweatshirt (the temperature having gone from forty degrees when I left the house, to somewhere near ninety, as is typical for Florida in November), I assumed at first that the smell came from me. However, this wasn't that type of smell. It was more like.... I didn't know, which was unusual for me. My nose usually knows.

I think something happens to a woman once she becomes a mother (besides the usual bags under the eyes from not sleeping and the urge to clean people's faces with her spit). Her senses become acutely tuned in to anything out of the ordinary. She can see through a child's lies and feel daggers coming from behind a closed door after a child's been sent to her room. She can taste a child's defeat as if it were her own and hear silent cries of fear and pain.

And she can smell trouble brewing a mile away.

My friend, Marti Attoun, once wrote a column about that very phenomenon: A mother's nose always knows. Probably at this very moment, a woman somewhere is sniffing the air and saying to herself, "There's a rotting piece of bologna on the second shelf of the refrigerator."

I think it starts with diapers, and that's all I'm going to say on that subject. Let's just say, a woman's olfactory glands become heightened from the day-to-day stimulation.

Maybe God made a woman's sense of smell so acute because he knew kids would instinctively ask their mothers, "Is chicken salad supposed to smell like this *before* or *after* it gets rotten?"

As a mother, I know what Play-Doh smells like when it has

been sitting on a radiator and how a wrapper from a contraband Snickers smells when hiding beneath a pile of wet towels under a bed. I can continue to smell permanent marker on a bedspread two full weeks after the marker's been capped and put back in my "don't touch" drawer. I know that a dog who's been fed leftover roast beef (that I'd hidden for a late night sandwich) smells happy and the one who did the feeding smells guilty, even before I ask, "Who ate the roast beef?"

With one sniff, I know who got into the M & M dispenser on my desk and who used flea powder as a "Barbie snow storm." I can even smell unfinished homework in a back pack.

The girls have often asked me how I know all these things. (They've long since accused me of having eyes in the back of my head, ears strategically tuned into every room in the house, and retractable arms that can grab the collar of someone on her way out the door, snap her back inside the house, snatch a bag of trash from the garage, and hand it to the escapee — all from the other side of the house.) I just tell them, "Mother Nose Best."

I took one more whiff of whatever smelled and knew right away: I smelled a ham sandwich on rye bread — with a dollop of mustard. The smell came from inside my car. By my best olfactory calculations, it had been there about a week, probably having been someone's lunch....'someone' who mistakenly confused my car with a trash can, that is.

"Whew! I have to get rid of that!" I said. I looked around and wondered about the possibility of a car thief coming to help me out...or an angel or an idea.

Since I didn't see anyone flapping his wings (and I didn't really want to run into a car thief), I decided to rely on an idea. So I sat down to wait for one to arrive.

I filed my nails. I hummed the score from *West Side Story*, I painted my toenails red. Then I remembered that those who lack wisdom are invited by God to ask and that He grants it freely.

I've asked God for wisdom plenty of times before, and He's always answered. When I'm at the market with only fifteen dollars to spend and near-empty cupboards at home, God directs me to the wisest buys when I ask. And then there are the times when the girls are sick. How does a mom know when it's serious enough to call the doctor? God knows, and He gives wisdom.

He's been our help when dealing with bullies on the school bus (sharing Tootsie Roll Pops works wonders), clashing schedules, flat tires, school-itis stomachaches, and much more.

However, until that day, I'd never asked God to help me break into a car. But He said to ask when we have needs, right?

Lord, I prayed, *uh, do You know how to pick a lock?*

That's when I thought about McGyver. In case you don't know who he is, he's a guy on TV who can get in (or out) of any situation with a bit of string, a broken pencil, a bent paper clip, a roll of duct tape, or an old bag of Cheetos.

With "What would McGyver do?" as my rallying cry, I searched the parking garage for something with which I could jimmy the lock. As luck would have it, I stumbled across a wire coat hanger, already opened and with a loop at the end (proving either I'm not the only one who locks their keys in the car, or that the airport parking lot truly is a car thief's paradise).

The secret, I knew from watching McGyver, is to sweat and grunt and wiggle the thing as the music intensifies, signaling impending doom. In the absence of climactic background music, I settled for sweating, grunting, and wiggling, eventually getting the door unlocked and the offensive sandwich removed.

How could I have missed that? I wondered. The odor of the mustard taunted me until — all traces of sentimentality purged from me — I let out a full, Tony the Tiger, "GRRRRRRRR!"

"Forget going home!" I cried. "I want to go to a place where leaving food in the car is a capital offense!"

I renewed my resolve to enjoy a much-needed getaway. But first, after all that sweating and grunting and leaning against my dirty car, I needed a bath.

"Surely God is my help; the Lord is the one who sustains me" (Psalm 54:4).

CHAPTER THIRTEEN

Rub-a-Dub-Dub, Mom's in the Tub

I NEEDED A BATH, or a reasonable facsimile thereof. Actually, I'd needed one for quite awhile. You see, as many times as I'd begged, "Calgon, take me away!" Calgon never did.

It's not that I haven't cleaned myself. It's just that, after all my years of motherhood, I've yet to have the bath of my dreams: the Calgon "take away" kind. Picture this: a sunken tub surrounded by ferns and greenery, filled with sudsing, milky white bubbles. You ease yourself into the ninety-two degree water and lay your head on a contour pillow that cradles your neck, then you sigh as Michael Bolton or Mozart or Garth Brooks or the Phantom of the Opera serenades you from your CD player. Not too loud, not too soft, and not the soundtrack from *Beauty and the Beast.*

You soap and soak and maybe even shave your legs or paint your toenails. You stay in the tub until your fingertips shrivel like raisins and you're good and ready to come out...and not one second before.

When you're finished, you discover warm, fluffy towels that are ample enough to wrap comfortably around your body. Also awaiting you is a frosted goblet of orange juice and a plate of Fig Newtons. Once the music ends and you brush Newton crumbs from your lips, you smile, because *that*, my dear, is a bath.

Unfortunately, the parking garage at the Orlando airport (although a fine a place, indeed) lacked the proper ambience — not to mention facilities — to accommodate my Bath of Dreams. The airport terminal, however, did have a ladies' room with sinks and water. I'd just have to make do with that. Besides, that's what mothers do: they make do.

Public bathrooms and I go way back. When I was little, my family would go out for Big Boy hamburgers and milkshakes. After we'd dumped ketchup in our laps, gotten cheese in our hair, and spilled milkshake down our shirts, Mom used to take me, my sister, and my two brothers into the bathroom, strip us down as far as the standards of decency would allow, and whip out a bar of soap from her purse.

She'd take a wash cloth (also from her purse), wet the four of us down — including our hair — soap us, then rinse us off, assembly-line style. Then she'd open her purse back up (Mom had an amazing purse), take out a towel to dry us off, then hand us each a change of clothes. After that we'd march out of the bathroom, our wet hair plastered to our faces, smelling of Ivory and whistling the theme to *The Bridge on the River Kwai* (which we knew as "The Malt-O-Meal Song").

When I had children of my own, I continued with the "public rest room as bathing facility" tradition set down by my mother. Of course, as a modern mother I was able to do away with having to carry huge bath towels around in my purse. With the invention of automatic hand dryers, I'd soap my kids down, rinse them off, then have them stand under the hot air in order to blow themselves dry. I had to give it up, though, when Laura started strip-ping off her clothes every time she went to use the bathroom at preschool and shouting, "Somebody hand me the shampoo, please!"

I trudged back into the airport, this time heading straight for the ladies' room. Once there, I opened up my suitcase, arranged my make-up and toiletries along the mirror ledge, and hung a fresh outfit on a stall door. Then, as I'd done as a child, I stripped down as far as the standards of decency would allow, filled the sink, and took the plunge into the sudsy water.

Like I said, I made do, but it definitely lacked the frosty O.J./plate of Fig Newtons/*Phantom of the Opera* serenade of my fantasy. *This just proves my theory of a cosmic conspiracy,* I thought as I rinsed off. *All we mothers want is privacy in the bathroom, but the laws of the universe prohibit it.*

As I scrunched underneath the hand dryer to blow myself dry, I let out another Tony the Tiger, "Grrrrrrr!" There I was: half-dressed in a public bathroom. Water was everywhere. I was squatting under a blast of hot air. People were walking around me, over me, and past me, shushing their children who asked, "Mom, why does that lady get to play with water, and I can't?" All this because I'd been deprived at home. Never mind that God said He'd supply all my needs. I thought He'd obviously overlooked this one.

I never thought I asked for much: Maybe that my favorite hairbrush not be used on the dog or end up tucked away in some-one's lunch box that's been left at school. Call me a nitpicker, but I've never liked having my eyeliner pencils used for homework or my nail file used to sharpen Popsicle sticks into spears. When I reach for a washcloth, I'd prefer one that hasn't already been used to wipe out the fish tank. And just once, when blow-drying my hair, I'd like to see only one face in the mirror: mine.

What is it about children and bathrooms? I pulled a T-shirt over my head and started to apply my make up at the bathroom mirror. All I knew was that a bathroom door closed longer than five minutes was reason for suspicion. Take a typical bathroom door conversation with Laura at age four:

"Laura, what are you doing in there?"

"Nothing."

"Can you unlock the door so Mommy can see?"

"Not yet. I'm busy."

"What are you busy doing?"

"Nothing."

In the past, I've discovered "nothing" to be two dozen unwrapped bars of soap, an entire roll of toilet paper unrolled into a heap on the floor, Vaseline smeared on the mirror, and a teddy bear taking a bubble bath in the toilet.

Those things I learned to live with. It was the combined sounds of flushing and giggling that caused me to panic. Echoes of: "Mommy, look at my shoe spin!" and "Bye-bye toothbrush!" still haunt me.

However, a four-year-old is nothing compared to an eight-year-old. An eight-year-old doing "nothing" in the bathroom is lying. Eight-year-olds shave their arms and try to pierce their own ears with a paper clip. They poke hundreds of tiny holes in the toothpaste tube and they cut their own hair — badly.

But at least eight-year-olds don't spend every waking moment in the bathroom like teenage girls do. When a teenage girl says she's doing "nothing" in the bathroom, she's doing exactly that — and it takes her an hour and a half to do it. Every hair has to be in place, every blemish on the face must be inspected...and cried over. Prayers must be offered up over a too-flat chest and too-wide hips.

When you ask, "What are you doing in there?" she replies, "Nothing! Can't everybody leave me alone?! Why are you always picking on me?"

When you ask her to open the door and she screams, "I'm too ugly, and I'm NEVER coming out!" believe her. She's never coming out.

That's why I've concluded that, as long as there are children living at home, mothers will never get the one thing they long for most (I mean besides sleep and a stick of margarine without finger holes punched in it). Mothers long most for a bath.

As I repacked all my things, I remembered the last bath I'd taken: January 13, 1973. That was before Magic Color-Change Donald Duck and Scrub-A-Dub Mickey® took over, before the Great Raspberry Jell-O Experiment, before bathtub ring and mildew on the ceiling.

Oh, I've tried taking a bath since then, but I've never actually succeeded. There seems to be a direct relationship between my foot hitting the water and a catastrophe on the other side of the bathroom door.

Once, in a moment of desperation, I left Barry with the girls and drove twenty miles to my sister's house. She was out of town for the weekend and I knew where she kept her spare key.

The entire way there, my heart pounded in anticipation of fragrant, silky bubbles. A real bath. All by myself. Alone.

My hopes were dashed as I rounded her corner and found the city workmen up to their ankles in water as they worked to fix a busted water main.

"Sorry, ma'am," said the one who flagged me down. "This street's closed and the water's shut off 'til tomorrow."

A forty-five minute drive and my hopes for a dream bath down the drain....

Yet another time, I was silly enough to try to take a bath no matter what. I announced to everyone, "I'm going to take a bath. All by myself. Alone." No sooner did I put my foot in the water then I heard a tiny knock-knock and the familiar words, "Mommy, I have to go potty."

Three minutes later, there was another knock. "Mom, you said you'd hem my skirt. Can you do it now?"

Another knock. "What are you doing in there?"

"Nothing. Go away."

They won't go away. I tried putting a Do Not Disturb sign on the door. They disturbed me. I locked the door. They picked the lock. I've pleaded, bargained, and threatened...all to no avail.

The last time I attempted to take a bath, I really thought I'd make it. I got as far as getting *both* feet in the tub before I heard a commotion outside the door.

"You ask her."

"Not me. You did it."

"Okay, we'll both ask. Uh, Mom, how do you put out a fire?"

I finished my sponge bath and let out a small sigh. Despite my frustration, I know in my heart that God provides everything I truly need. Maybe it's not the bath I need so much as it is the cleansing.

"Okay, God," I said as I put the rest of my things back into my suitcase. "I give myself up to You. Make me clean *Your* way." Still, I couldn't resist one last suggestion:

"But bubbles *would* be nice!"

"But you were washed, you were sanctified, you were justified in the name of the Lord Jesus Christ and by the Spirit of our God" (1 Corinthians 6:11).

CHAPTER FOURTEEN

I've Never Met a Bathing Suit I Didn't Hate

WITH RENEWED DETERMINATION and a clean face, I carried my suitcase and my anticipation of an adventure Somewhere Else toward Ticket Agent Blake's smiling face.

I'd read in the book of Psalms that the psalmist loved the place where God's glory dwells, and that's where I wanted to go. I'd never had it pointed out to me on a map. I didn't have a clue as to where it might be. Nevertheless, I'd decided it was where I was headed.

Wherever it was, it surely had a bathtub for every mother who wanted one and goblets of frosty orange juice at a woman's beck and call. Not to mention jars of crisp kosher dill pickles that actually have pickles left in them at the end of the week, bottomless containers of spicy mustard, self-folding laundry, and *no* cries of "Just five more minutes, please Mom?!"

As the line inched forward, I continued daydreaming. Then a

little voice inside my head suggested, "There's no place like home; there's no place like home."

Listen, Voice, I argued, *that may have worked for Dorothy in the Land of Oz, but I don't see any ruby slippers on my feet.* I clicked the heels of my Reeboks to prove it.

The voice took another tack, this time whispering, "Home is where the heart is, and where your heart is, that's where your treasure will be."

OK, but home is also where people cut out current events before anyone has a chance to read the newspaper. Home is where people laugh at a person's rendition of "Don't Cry for Me, Argentina" while she's singing on the treadmill. Home is where people press their noses on the front window and get the telephones and door knobs greasy. Home is where the request to clean your room is treated as grounds for child abuse.

My turn in line came up just as the voice started to sing, "Turn your heart towards home..."

"Well, nice to see you again!" said Blake as he clicked his pen. "Did you decide on where you're headed?"

"Surprise me," I said. "Just make it someplace glorious."

"How about the Bahamas?" he suggested. "Easy to spell — B-A-H-A-M-A-S — tropical weather. I hear it's paradise."

I could handle paradise. I mulled it over. Palm trees, coconut seven-layer cake, white sandy beaches, dark-haired natives with unpronounceable names bringing me fresh kiwis and pineapple spears....

Blake pointed to a photo of happy Bahama-ites in a travel brochure. "Mrs. Kennedy, you wouldn't even have to do laundry. All you'd need is a bathing suit and a smile."

"Excuse me," I said, shaking my head in disbelief. "Did you say bathing suit?"

Obviously this young man's mother never taught him to refrain from using the "B" word to a person of the maternal persuasion.

The women in the crowd behind me alternately cringed, cried, stared blankly into space, and laughed uncontrollably at mental images of their Jell-O-like bodies being crammed into a half-a-yard of Lycra spandex. As my friend Pam describes it, trying to get a post-pregnancy body into a bathing suit is on a par with trying to get a cranky, lock-lipped toddler to eat one more bite of beets. It ain't gonna work. And even if it did, the results would not be a pleasant sight.

The truth is, even though our husbands say we're beautiful and our children don't seem to care, once a woman has children, she can *never* wear a bathing suit again. At least not unself-consciously.

This poses a problem because the very children who cause our "excessive adiposal condition" are also the ones who beg us to take them swimming. Thus, the dilemma. Do we maintain our dignity safely underneath baggy sweats and oversized T-shirts and deny our children a day in the water, or do we expose our shortcomings, downfalls, potbellies, and cellulite in order to provide our children with aquatic knowledge and perhaps lifesaving water skills?

Tough choice.

I, for one, held out as long as I could. I remember it well. One day during *Oprah* ("Women whose thighs look like cottage cheese-stuffed manicotti and the families who love them"), the phone rang. It was my single and childless friend Melissa (the one with only one stomach, and a flat one at that), announcing the arrival of summer with a suggestion that it was time I teach my daughter to swim.

Now, there comes a time when a baby needs to be water-safe,

and (since Alison was about to graduate high school and Laura had just turned twelve) I decided I'd waited long enough. The problem was, I didn't have a you-know-what (the B-word), and the thought of shopping for one made my stretch marks itch and my legs break out in a rash.

Melissa, dear sweet Melissa (who thinks that stretch marks are the red indentations she gets around her ankles from her sport socks), wouldn't hear any of my excuses. "Just zip over to Teeny's Weeny Bikinis where I shop and pick up a suit. How hard can that be?"

First of all, I lost my zip years ago somewhere between 2:00 A.M. feedings and potty training. Secondly, after bearing two children, I seriously doubt any store with the words "teeny" or "weeny" in its name would have anything suitable for me. Instead, I tried the Miracle Workers-R-Us shop at the mall.

Armed with an ounce of hope and several fashion magazines with lists of bathing suit do's and don'ts for every figure flaw, I sucked in all of my stomachs and marched inside.

Hope — and everything else — gave way to gravity as soon as I saw a poster on the wall of bikini-clad models lying on a sandy beach. Not a stretch mark or a spare tire in the bunch. In a moment of panic, I tried closing my eyes and willing myself thin and beautiful, to no avail. I needed a miracle.

Now, I know that the Bible says I am fearfully and wonderfully made. Unfortunately, I'm also abundantly, plentifully, amply, generously, and liberally made. I'm what is, at my house, called "shapely." (One day as Laura inspected me while I got dressed, she commented that my legs were "kinda fat." I corrected her by saying, "My legs aren't fat. They're shapely." She replied, "Then they're the shapeliest legs I've ever seen.")

I stood in the store amid racks of garments no bigger than postage stamps, clinging to a vague hope that not only would one of them fit, but I would actually look good wearing it.

After grabbing several industrial strength-looking suits and heading for the dressing room, I immediately lowered my expectations from "fit and look good" to "won't make me wish the earth would open up and swallow me."

Following all the magazines' rules for my *anjou* body (that means pear-shaped, but I've always thought *anjou* sounded thinner), I tried on a suit with a high cut leg that "they" claim makes wide hips look longer, thus creating the illusion of leanness.

"They" were wrong. The high cut leg on my hips created no illusion whatsoever. Not only that, my legs had nowhere to hide. They were just there. Uncovered. Bare. I could already hear the comments from tanned, zinc-nosed lifeguards at the pool as they pointed and announced via bullhorn, "Look at the way that lady jiggles when she walks."

Next, I tried on a "boy-leg" cut, sort of like shorts attached to a tank top. Theoretically, this style should be the most flattering since it covers the most skin, but theory rarely matches reality. In the real world of soft, pliable maternal flesh, the boy leg covers the hips and some of the thigh but it doesn't go quite far enough down the leg. There's always left-over leg hanging out that no one seems to know what to do with. And no matter how hard you try to stuff it back inside the suit, the leftover leg still looks like a big piece of cauliflower sticking out of an upside-down blue tube.

I settled on the third suit I tried on. It was the style Melissa refers to as a "Miss America," but with its built-in bra, tummy control panel, belly-hiding sash, and saddlebag-disguising skirt, I deemed it...well, adequate. Although I shuddered to think it's the same style my 62-year-old mother wears, at least it met my criteria: It fit, it pushed me in where I want to be in and up where I normally sag, and the sight of me in it didn't make me want to throw up, cry, or both.

I still haven't worn it to the pool.

The bottom line is (no pun intended), the sags and bags and hips the size of Kansas that stay with you until your baby is eligible for Medicare are much like death and taxes. Can't do much about them, either.

However, there's hope. Someday God is going to give us all new bodies. Personally, I'm hoping for one like Melissa's, but I'll settle for an average size ten, preferably with a flat stomach and hips without saddlebags. Add to that list thighs that don't jiggle (or cause kids to giggle) when I walk.

Meanwhile, I think I'll settle for finding a suit with maximum coverage and rejoicing in a God who happens to think I'm beautiful: bulges, ripples, and all.

"I praise you because I am fearfully and wonderfully made" (Psalm 139:14).

CHAPTER FIFTEEN

Night Night, Sleep Tight (Yeah, *Right*)

LOOK IT UP in your *Roget's Thesaurus*. The word "mother" is synonymous with tired. And I was tired. Nineteen year's worth of tired to be exact. I knew I didn't want to wear a you-know-what every day in the Bahamas, but I was too tired to choose another destination. I grabbed a handful of travel brochures from the rack on the counter next to Blake and excused myself one more time.

"I'll just (yawn) step over here (yawn) and consider my (yawn) options," I told him, and pushed my suitcase over to a nearby bench.

I sat down and leaned my head against the wall to think. As I closed my eyes, I pictured myself lying in a hammock underneath two oak trees, swaying to a warm, gentle breeze. Not that I'd ever done that, mind you. But I've often thought about it, lusted over it, talked about it in great detail with my friends.

My mother and her friends used to do that, too. I remember

the first time I stumbled upon The Conversation. I was about fourteen. Mom and her friends were sitting around the kitchen table drinking strong coffee when one of them began, "Here's how I picture it: A soft feather bed, crisp white sheets, and I'm dressed in satin — no, make that cotton as soft as down."

Then another broke in with, "The lights dim, and the anticipation makes your heart race."

A third added, "No music. Just silence. Delicious silence."

About that time I sneezed or something. The women, startled by the intrusion, abruptly changed the subject to the upcoming PTA bowl-a-thon.

For years I thought they'd been discussing romantic fantasies. Of course, now I know differently. My mother and her friends had been talking about Sleep. Glorious, precious, elusive sleep. The Holy Grail of motherhood. The Ultimate Pleasure. The Big Kahuna.

As my mother and her friends before me, my friends and I discuss and compare past enjoyed and future anticipated sleep experiences as wine connoisseurs discuss the heady bouquets of vintage wines. It's a clear case of "Those who can, do. Those who can't, make up elaborate fantasies." It's virtual reality without all the technology.

Husbands don't understand this preoccupation, this borderline worshipful state of desire, over sleep. As Barry says, "What's the big deal? The ten o'clock news guy signs off, you turn out the light and — boom! — at six the alarm goes off." He still believes the large, bedspread-covered, multi-pillowed piece of furniture in our bedroom is a place of rest and relaxation.

And why shouldn't he? He's successfully slept through every nocturnal trauma (real or imagined), every whimper, sneeze, cough, nightmare, and midnight rumination over the probability of snakes dropping on a kid's head through the heater vent.

Kids don't understand a mother's single-minded obsession either. Kids fight to ward off bedtime; mothers fight to experience it. Kids think sleep is a necessary evil and a bore. Even if they can't keep their eyes open, they'll beg to stay up "just one more hour."

They don't know what they're missing. But then, that's the whole point — they're not missing anything. They can have all they want. The trouble is, they've never wanted it. They've never had TMS (Tired Mother Syndrome), either.

There's a woman at my church who has five or six kids. She has chronic TMS. The other day I saw her sitting in her station wagon in the library parking lot coloring in a Bugs Bunny coloring book. When I asked her what she was doing, she answered, "Cooking dinner."

I understood completely.

Now, she's a reasonably intelligent woman. She fully understood that she was, in fact, not cooking dinner but waiting for her oldest child to check out a library book. It just came out, "Cooking dinner."

I tried explaining it to my childless friend, Melissa, several years ago when she asked me how I liked Mel Gibson and I answered, "Sunny-side up." (I meant to say, "Hubba hubba.") I'd been up and down a dozen times the night before. (Why is it that whenever a child can't sleep she feels the need to wake Mom up for regular updates every fifteen minutes?) I suffered an acute case of TMS that day, the first sign being brain scrambling. It's a direct result of your head not spending enough quality bonding time with your pillow, which in turn makes your "Hubba hubbas" come out "Sunny-side up."

Another sign, as exhibited by my friend from church, is pew slumbering. This woman is the first to rave about our pastor's preaching. She's always praising the choir, and she thinks the drama team is the greatest. Little does she know, she's never seen or heard any of them on a Sunday morning. The minute she gets all her little ones settled in the nurseries and children's church, she takes her usual seat way in the back, immediately falls asleep, and stays that way until the final Amen. Then, as she makes her way through the parking lot, she tells everyone how refreshing she found the service.

I remember my first pew slumbering episode. Only it wasn't in a padded wooden pew, but in a folding metal chair. I'd been up all night with a teething Alison, rubbing Anbesol on her gums and wondering about the world's record for the longest consecutive number of sleepless nights — and whether I'd surpassed it.

(Note: The world's record currently belongs to my friend from church — 4,387 nights in a row.)

The next day was Sunday. I walked into the eleven o'clock service, my shirt on inside out (TMS sign #3), my skirt wrinkled because...well, because I was too tired to iron it and I figured, "Hey, at least I'm dressed" (TMS sign #4).

I flopped down onto my metal chair in my usual place in the front row. Then, just as the pastor stood up to welcome the congregation, my head flew backwards and I let out a resounding snort.

Now, I don't usually make a habit of snoring. However, I firmly believe that if you're going to do something, you should do it with all your might. So I did. In front of God and everybody, I snored at the top of my lungs and in harmony with the choir as they sang, "O for a Thousand Tongues." Eventually someone tipped me over (which stopped my snoring, I'm pleased to say), spread a jacket over me, and put a hymnal under my head. This allowed me — and everyone around me — to enjoy the rest of the service. I don't remember the pastor's sermon, but I do remember it being the most refreshing service I'd ever attended.

I always thought (mistakenly) I'd get to sleep once the kids got older, that TMS is a temporary condition. It's a common misconception among TMS sufferers. You tell yourself from day one, "As soon as she sleeps through the night I'll get some sleep (TMS sign #5). When that day comes — three years later — you and your husband celebrate, but then nine months later you're up all night once again.

My friend, Melissa, often thinks she's tired. She'll say something like, "Oh, wow! I'm, like, sooo tired. I stayed up reading this really, really good book until way past midnight and I still had to get up at 7:00 A.M.! It was so grueling, I had to veg out on the couch for an hour after work."

"Melissa," I'll say, "That's not tired. Tired is being up since 4:00 A.M. and not stopping once during the day. It's not getting a shower until noon and it's watching Jay Leno say good night while you're still up nursing a baby who's just getting her second wind and wants to party. Tired is finally getting her to sleep, then hearing the alarm go off before you even get back into bed. Tired is having to shoo monsters from a toddler's closet at 2:00 A.M. and standing in the hallway for eight hours straight, listening to the labored breathing of a child with a stuffy nose. Tired is encountering at midnight a frantic middle schooler who forgot to wash her gym clothes. Tired is waiting until you hear the front door being opened by your high schooler who's been out with the car. That's tired."

My friend Melissa still doesn't understand, although authr

Melissa Fay Greene does. She wrote once that she's developed a motto: Whenever life presents you with a multiple choice situation in which sleep is one of the answers, choose sleep.

For example, if you can either: (a) be rich, powerful, beautiful, and successful or (b) sleep, the obvious answer is (b).

However, on those occasions in which sleep isn't an option, I propose another option: reciting Psalm 121:3. "He who watches over you will not slumber; indeed, he who watches over Israel will neither slumber nor sleep."

I've discovered that the quiet hours of the night are often the times when God's whispers can be heard most clearly as I recall His Word that I've hidden in my heart: "Come to me, all you who are weary and burdened, and I will give you rest" (Matthew 11:28). "Cast all your anxiety on him because he cares for you" (1 Peter 5:6). "My soul finds rest in God alone" (Psalm 62:1).

So, next time you're up before dawn nursing a baby, chasing monsters from the closet, changing wet sheets, or washing gym clothes, keep in mind that the God of the Universe is also awake. As long as you have to be up, at least you can know you're in the best company.

If you listen closely, you may even hear Him whispering a bedtime story.

"He gives power to the tired and worn out, and strength to the weak" (Isaiah 40:29 LB).

CHAPTER SIXTEEN

"Oops" Is Just Another Word for "Go Get a Mop"

STILL ON THE BENCH, still leaning my head against the wall, I was still undecided as to my runaway destination. The truth is I didn't know where to go, mainly because I'd never been anywhere before. At least not by myself. In all my forty years, I'd never traveled without my mom and dad, my aunt, or my husband and children.

In my fantasies, however (as I'm battling lime deposit in the shower or desperately seeking the mates to single socks), I'm a first-class world traveler. I imagine myself bustling through busy airports, hailing taxis on metropolitan streets, renting my own rental cars, tipping bell boys at posh hotels. Picture a shorter, rounder version of Mary Tyler Moore. I've got the squeaky voice and I can toss my hat up in the air like she does, but that's about it.

Come to think of it, I did travel alone once. Sort of.

When I was nineteen, I joined the air force. Uncle Sam made all my travel arrangements, putting me up at no-star barracks where I dined on gooey stuff over rice and drank strong black coffee, but I did have to get on a plane all by myself. I traveled to exotic places like Limestone, Maine, and San Antonio, Texas.

I could go to Denver, I thought, but I rejected that idea: too cold at that time of year. That also ruled out Saginaw, Green Bay, and Lake Woebegone, not to mention the rest of the northern half of the United States and most of the eastern seaboard.

As my list of destination choices narrowed, so did my eyes. In fact, they even closed — but not for long. Just as I started to doze off, a loud, "Oops!" jolted me awake.

Instinctively, I cried, "Go get a mop!"

But it wasn't a "Go Get a Mop" Oops. This was an "I Can't Believe I Did That" Oops and it came from a young man racing down the airport who'd just committed a hit-and-run incident involving an older man's briefcase, the contents of which were now spread across the airport lobby.

"Oops!" is an expression I'm intimately acquainted with, having heard and said it more times than I care to count. It's a popular word at my house.

The child who stuffed Tinker Toys down the toilet uttered it when she went to flush and all the wooden sticks and round things got stuck, causing the water to back up. I said it after Barry, home on his lunch break, took the whole thing up off the floor, set it in the bathtub, went back to work, and left me home with a full bladder and no second bathroom to use. This led me to run next door to finally meet my neighbor, at which point I locked myself out of the house. Oops.

Laura said it the time she went to shake a paper bag off of a bottle of cranberry juice and accidentally let go of the bottle top, causing the bottle to sail across the floor like a bowling ball and crash against the kitchen wall.

I've oopsed over using liquid dish soap in the dishwasher when the powdered stuff ran out. (Note: Don't do this unless you like bubbles cascading out the sides of the dishwasher door and across the kitchen floor.) I've oopsed over mistaking flea spray for air freshener.

If you ask Barry, he'd say he never oopses, but he does. Every night, in fact. At around eight o'clock he grabs a bowl of ice cream, which he insists he can eat only while sitting on our bed. He's learned to drape a towel over his lap, but every night he somehow misses. And every night around 8:05 I hear him say, "Oops! Sorry, hon!"

In addition to individual oopsing, we also have moments of familial oopsing. Our most memorable was several years ago on Thanksgiving. We had started a tradition of going to the movies, then to a local restaurant for their Thanksgiving buffet. That year's movie was *Home Alone 2,* and as we critically tore it apart on the way to the restaurant, Barry casually asked me if I was sure the place was open.

"Don't be ridiculous!" I said. "Of course they're open."

Oops.

When we got there, we found all the lights out and all the chairs stacked on the tables. The girls and Barry ended up eating Burger King fare, and I ate crow. Of course, it wasn't entirely my fault. That's why I consider this a familial oops — nobody else thought to call the restaurant either. So there.

I oopsed a lot as a child. I committed the unpardonable (at least according to my dad) sin of putting the hamburger meat on the homemade pizza before the cheese. I lured every cat in the neighborhood into my garage and fed it until they all decided our casa was their casa and they all clawed holes in the window screens. Once I tried storing one of my grandmother's fudge cakes under my bed so my brothers couldn't eat it. It gathered ants from as far away as Reno, Nevada. I didn't do anything about it until my mom found it several weeks later. By then there were other, rodent-type life forms involving themselves in the chocolate orgy, and Mom was none too pleased. Oops.

I always thought I'd outgrow my propensity toward oopsing, but unfortunately for my children, I haven't. Much to their horror, I've actually increased my maternal oopsing activity.

I once stumbled upon a piece of paper that had initials doodled all over it (initials which I cannot divulge or I will be guilty of the Mother of all Oopses), written in the handwriting of one of my daughters. I deduced they belonged to a boy, and as any concerned mother would do, I looked through my daughter's yearbook for telltale signs: a happy face, a star, an "I Love You!!!" written underneath a name. I found zip.

Next I went down the list of every boy in her grade, looking for one with those initials. (I found three.) Using the scientific method (closing my eyes and randomly selecting one with my finger), I landed on _____ (remember, I can't say his name), who just happened to be the son of a friend of mine and a very nice boy at that (or so says my friend). And since my daughter (who shall remain nameless so I can protect my neck) hadn't mentioned him ever, I thought it would be a nice gesture to invite him and his family over for a barbecue.

That's when I discovered nice gestures equal bedroom doors slamming in your face and "How could you!" echoing in your ear. As it turned out, the initials didn't belong to my friend's son but to some television hunk of the month. During the barbecue with my friend and her family, my daughter and the boy sat on opposite sides of the table and didn't say one word to each other...or to anyone else for that matter. The rest of us had a great time as my friend and I serenaded everyone with "Love Is a Many Splendored Thing" while we flipped burgers onto the grass.

Although matchmaking barbecues rank high in the annals of motherhood oopses, my biggest oopses have involved misplacing or forgetting my children. When Alison was still in high school, I always managed to forget to pick her up. With irregular after-school meetings, I waited at the wrong gate, came the wrong day, or didn't come at all (until after she'd waited an hour and had to convince the janitor to let her in to use the office phone). She used to tape signs to my steering wheel: "PLEASE!!!!! PICK ME UP!!!!!! 5:00!!!!! EAST GATE!!!!! PLEASE!!!!!"

Forgetting Alison at age eighteen, although inexcusable, is not as bad as forgetting a three-year-old Laura at a diner. The girls and I had been on the road, traveling to my aunt's house. At that age, Laura only knew one speed at which to talk: mega non-stop. That day, she was particularly driving me crazy by yakking about her brand new My Little Pony and how she wanted to feed it oats, and Mom, we have to stop for some oats 'cause the pony blah, blah, blah, and if we don't stop for oats the pony's going to get hungry and blah, blah, blah, blah, blah.

So, we stopped for oats, or at least a soda, at a diner. On the way out, I made a deal with Laura: if she could stay in the back seat, remaining absolutely quiet the rest of the way to Aunt

Gladys's, she could ride up front on the way home and tell me all about her pony. We shook on it, then left for a peaceful ride.

When we got to my aunt's, I turned around to commend Laura on keeping her part of the agreement, and discovered — no Laura. My heart stopped beating and didn't start up again until, after breaking every known traffic law, I pulled into the parking lot of the diner, raced through the door, and found my sweet Laura, wearing a paper chef's hat and an apron, spinning around on a counter stool and eating a banana split. When she saw me, all she said was, "Hi, Mom! I'm a waitress!"

I could sit here for days listing all the oopses of my life, I thought as I shifted my weight on the airport bench and fanned through the pile of travel brochures. I'm just glad God never says, "Oops!"

All the mistakes I've made, all the messes I've gotten in, all the joys as well as sorrows, the pain, the suffering, the rectangular birthmark on the back of my leg — even the time I stood up to give an oral report in the fourth grade and threw up — all that, He has ordained for me in order that I might be conformed into the likeness of His Son.

I don't even try to understand it; I just place my limited faith in His limitless wisdom and in His promise to work everything in my life for good.

Even the time I accidentally glued myself to the garage floor.

"Many are the plans in a man's heart, but it is the LORD's purpose that prevails" (Proverbs 19:21).

CHAPTER SEVENTEEN

I'd Tell You Why Motherhood Makes Women Absentminded, But I Forget

ONCE AGAIN, I leaned my head back against the wall in order to take a snooze. However, just as I closed my eyes, a nagging thought jarred me awake.

I'd forgotten something.

I knew I had my clothes and the TV remote control. I had my entire life's savings and a supply of breath mints. I even had a current issue of People magazine with Princess Di on the cover.

Did I turn off the stove? I wondered. *Feed the cats?* I looked down at my shoes. One time when I'd gone to buy shoes for

Laura, I left the house and forgot to check if I had on a matching pair. I wandered around the store wearing one white Reebok with blue trim and one white Nike with a black "swoosh." I couldn't figure out why the salesman kept looking at me feet and asking if I needed help.

My shoes match, so that's not it. It's not my watch or earrings or lipstick. As I sat there taking inventory of myself, I remembered. However, I didn't remember what I thought I had forgotten; I remembered the time Alison stuck a popcorn seed up her nose and it sprouted. I remembered the year she was five and had night terrors. Every single night, exactly one hour after she had fallen asleep, she would wake up and run, wild-eyed, through the house, crying, "Mommy! Mommy! Mommy!" about a hundred times.

I remembered the time I flushed a bucket of squid down the toilet and it wouldn't stay down, and the "hairy eyeball" — a blue marble stuck in the brick wall on Chase Street — that was rumored to bring evil to anyone passing directly in front of it on the way to and from Nevada Avenue Elementary School.

I remembered my white go-go boots, being in love with Mickey Dolenz of the Monkees, and the time in junior high that I insisted on wearing a rust-colored corduroy jumper with hot pink tights...but I couldn't remember what I'd forgotten. This really didn't surprise me; I'd gotten used to being forgetful. I could remember things from my childhood, but ask me what I fixed for dinner last night and I draw a blank.

I once read a magazine article about postpartum amnesia. It quoted experts as saying the reason motherhood makes women absentminded has to do with the hormones oxytocin, estrogen, and thyroxine being out of whack. This makes sense when you're a new mother who can't remember her address without reading it off the mailbox or who mechanically puts the carton of ice cream in the file cabinet. Eventually the hormones level out. The problem of forgetting which breast you left off with the last time you nursed remedies itself when you get tired of being lopsided, and you learn to write your name on your hand to remind yourself who you are. But when your baby drives off to college in her new car, you really can't blame postpartum anything on the fact that you still need a note to remind you to pick up the dry cleaning before the cleaner's goes out of business.

I have my own theory concerning motherhood forgetfulness. I believe it's due to brain overload. Take the average mother of three children. Throughout the course of a day she has to know who goes to what school, who needs lunch money and who hates cafeteria macaroni and cheese, who has soccer practice on Field B, and whose practice is at the elementary school. She has to know that Daughter A needs a pair of black tights for dance class, Daughter B has a teeth cleaning appointment at 4:30, the chicken needs to go in the oven at 4:15, and there's no toilet paper in the hall bathroom. She maintains the supply of trash bags, razor blades, and Band-Aids, knows that canned goods are at least five cents cheaper at Store X than Store Y, and has everyone's social security number, shoe size, and Christmas list memorized.

A few years ago when I went to a five-day conference, Barry took time off from work to be Mr. Mom. Before I left, I wrote out a list of everything that had to be done: Pick Laura and her friends, Kelly and Melanie, up from school at 2:55 (park on the left side facing east); then drop Melanie off at her brother's day care; then take Kelly home; then pick Alison up at 3:10 (park on the street by the cafeteria). Laura has cheerleading practice at five, and Alison needs to be at work at five, so take Alison first, etc., etc.

You get the picture.

Later, when I called home, Barry wailed into the phone, "You wouldn't believe all the things I had to do today!" Then he counted off about five of the more than twenty (bare minimum) things I had listed. And forget about cooking; he ordered pizza all five nights I was away.

As forgetful as I am, I didn't forget to remind him I do all that (and then some) every day…without crib notes.

The daily routine stuff I rarely forget, but if you add a new variable (such as having to pick someone up at a later time), my circuits get crossed, my gray matter reaches its saturation point, and I suffer brain overload.

To remedy the situation, and to keep brain seepage to a minimum, I've devised a selective forgetfulness plan. For example: there are several things I plan to forget one day, such as the time a family member (who shall remain anonymous) took a piece of bread and wiped spaghetti sauce off her face — then ate the bread. "People sop up sauce on their plate," she reasoned. "Why not sauce on the face?"

I plan to forget the time I permed my hair a bit too tightly. Nobody said anything until a little girl in church turned around, looked at me, and announced, "Look, Mommy! That lady looks like Grandma's poodle!"

I plan on forgetting the words to every Raffi song ("Goin' on a picnic, leavin' right away; if it doesn't rain…"), every knock-knock joke ("Knock-knock. Who's there? Boo. Boo Who? Aww, don't cry."), every episode of *Full House*.

In a few years, I'll no longer remember how to do "My-mother-your-mother-lived-across-the-street…" hand clapping games or that Malibu Barbie gets the hot pink bathing suit and Superstar Barbie gets the evening gown. I won't even remember whether or not Sam I Am likes green eggs and ham.

Some things, though, are indelibly etched in my memory. I will never forget wheeling four-year-old Alison down the crowded pet supplies aisle when she sighed (loudly) and asked, "Mom, do we *have* to eat dog food again tonight?"

I'll also never forget how she cured me (temporarily) from complaining about doing laundry. After about seven years of hearing, "All I ever do is laundry around here!" Alison devised a way to ease my load: she'd throw her underwear away instead of putting it in the hamper. However, there was one flaw in her logic, which she discovered after about a week when she went to get dressed for a Brownie field trip.

Around seven one Saturday morning, she came into my room and told me she didn't have any underwear.

"That's ridiculous," I replied. "Everyone in this family has underwear."

She looked at me and said, "I don't."

"Well, what happened to it?"

"I don't know."

"Did you have any yesterday?"

"Yes."

"What happened to those?"

"I don't know."

This line of questioning went on until I decided to search the house myself. Sure enough, she was right: no underwear anywhere. And she had to get dressed and to her Brownie outing by 9:30.

After repeatedly urging her, "Come on, I won't get mad —

just tell me where your underwear went," I finally got Alison to confess.

We got the story out in the open and I kept my promise not to get mad, but that didn't change the fact that she still didn't have any underwear to wear (except for the pair she'd thrown away the night before). We dug that pair out of the trash with the plan that I'd wash them in the sink and put them in the dryer so Alison could be ready in time.

I thought it was a foolproof idea; I didn't count on the dryer conking out.

I went to Plan B.

I remembered my mom used to take our wet shoes and put them in the oven to dry off. I figured: *Shoes — underwear, what's the difference?*

I preheated the oven to 350 degrees, spread out her panties on a cookie sheet, set the timer for twenty minutes, then went to get myself dressed.

Twenty minutes passed. *Ding!* The timer went off, Alison and I raced into the kitchen, and she asked, "Are they dry, Mom?" I lifted up the charred remains (the rest having crumbled to the floor).

Our eyes grew wide and our mouths dropped open as we stared at Fruit of the Loom dust all over the kitchen.

"Yep," I told her. "They're dry."

I ended up driving all over the county for the next hour, trying to find a store that sold little girls' underwear that was open on a Saturday morning. We found one at nine, Alison made it to her Brownie outing in time, and from then on, I've used cookie sheets only for baking cookies.

Yes, because I'm a mother, my brain hovers dangerously

close to overload; however, I'll always have room to remember these things:

• God's grace is amazing and sufficient for my every need. I'll never forget our year of unemployment when I was pregnant with Laura. In ways we still don't understand, God allowed us to pay all our bills and still have money left over.

• The same power God used to raise Christ from the dead is available to me through the indwelling Holy Spirit (Ephesians 1:18ff). Although tired, I still manage to survive sleepless nights and function the next day. When sick myself, I've been able to nurse the other family members who were down with the flu. This power enables me to stretch and bend in ways I never thought possible. It enables me to endure the times a child screams, "I hate you!" and to stand firm in my discipline. It enables me to live a life of holiness.

• I am created for God's glory (Isaiah 43:7) and for his pleasure (Revelation 4:11 KJV). He takes great delight in me, quiets me with His love, and rejoices over me with singing (Zephaniah 3:17). Whenever past failures haunt me or I'm overcome by fears of the future, I think of God singing because of me and am encouraged. His love lifts me and casts out all my fear.

• Someday I shall see Jesus.

 Oh…and one last thing:

• Underwear is better air-dried than charbroiled.

"I will remember the deeds of the LORD.…I will meditate on all your works and consider all your mighty deeds" (Psalm 77:11-12).

Those Three Little Words

I HADN'T LEFT the bench I'd been sitting on; I was still trying to remember what I'd forgotten. My green eyeliner pencil? My tube of under-eye dark-circle cover? My fuzzy blue socks that I wear to bed when Barry's gone?

And then it hit me.

Right there, right in the middle of the Orlando airport — in front of God and the man sweeping up gum wrappers, the businessmen in their gray suits and red ties, and even the nun glancing through a *Reader's Digest* — I let out a whimper.

I'd forgotten how much I loved hearing those "three little words," and I longed to hear them once again.

I let out another whimper as I thought back to the last time I'd heard them. It was a Monday morning. The early morning moonlight streamed through the cracks in our bedroom blinds, and the faint strains of music from the clock radio gently nudged me awake. Barry, noticing me stirring, propped himself up on his elbow. Leaning over me, he brushed the hair from my cheek and greeted me with those three little words that still get my heart racing and my temperature rising.

"Back to school," he whispered.

I savored the phrase, turning it over and over in my mind. "Say it loud and there's music playing; say it soft and it's almost like praying...."

Don't get me wrong. I love my kids, but I also love my sanity, and by the end of August, I usually run out just about the time Laura starts her "Why can't I make a water slide off the garage roof?" campaign.

Back to school. I love everything about it. I love the shopping and the smell of unworn socks straight from the package. I love the sound of the school bus squealing its tires, the feel of the front door as I close it behind the last one out, and the taste of solitude.

Laura once asked me what solitude tasted like, so I told her: chocolate-chip cookie-dough ice cream. The girls have always accused me of eating ice cream for breakfast when they're not home, and the truth is...they're right. I do everything they think I do, and then some.

Each first day of school, the number one item on my agenda (after eating the ice cream) is to try on all their new clothes. Of course, I've only been able to do this for the past five years or so. Before that I'd play with all their toys and draw happy faces on their chalk boards.

Next, I jump on their beds. Our friend Peter waited until his children were grown, married, and living in their own homes before he jumped on their beds. But I say, "Why wait?"

After I jump (and sing all ten verses of "No more monkeys jumpin' on the beds"), I usually ride one of their bikes to McDonald's and slide down the slide in the play area, or I take a trek to

Disney World and spin on the tea cups ride until my eyeballs fall out. Next, I come home for more ice cream and an hour of cartoons. Then just about the time the school bus squeals around the corner, I tie on an apron, grab a dust rag, put on a haggard face, and assume my position on top of the step ladder, swiping at cobwebs.

My mom had her own "back to school" rituals. Early in the morning we'd hear her sigh as only a mother of four children can sigh after spending ninety-plus long, hot days of summer vacation refereeing four-way squabbles over who gets the last Popsicle in the freezer, chauffeuring in umpteen directions simultaneously, and entertaining us: the unentertainable and the chronically bored.

After she'd sigh, she'd sprint downstairs, uncharacteristically alert for such an early hour, to fix us A Good Breakfast. This was back in the sixties when A Good Breakfast consisted of bacon, eggs (cooked to order), juice, toast, and milk. That's what she fixed on Day One.

On Day Two, she'd come downstairs a little slower and we'd find a pan full of scrambled eggs on the stove and the milk carton on the table alongside a loaf of bread and the toaster. Day Three would bring money on the table accompanied by a note: "Stop at the donut shop before school."

On Days Four and Five we'd usually find just a note that read: "Today we're fasting."

But on Day One, Mom was in rare form. She'd see that our "days of the week" underwear were correct ("You can't wear your Saturdays on Monday! What if you get in an accident? What will the hospital think?"). She'd see that my pixie haircut had the proper amount of Dippity Do to make my bangs stay in place (i.e., glued to my head), that my sister's pig tails were tight enough to pull at her temples and cause her severe neck pain, and that my brothers had on enough Brill Cream ("a little dab'll do ya") to give them that Beaver Cleaver look.

We were never sure what Mom did after she double-knotted our orthopedic saddle shoes (also popular in the sixties), handed us each our Quick Draw McGraw or Huckleberry Hound lunch boxes, cleaned our faces with her thumb and spit, and waved good-bye from the front door, but she always seemed happy to see us walk off toward the goal of higher education.

Now that I'm a mother, I know better. As soon as we rounded the corner, she whipped out the ice cream, drew happy faces on our chalk boards, and jumped on our beds.

In our area of Florida, there's a television commercial for an office supply chain that shows a dad almost flying through the store, pushing a shopping cart, a huge smile on his face as he loads up on school supplies, while two kids trudge behind him. In the background, Andy Williams is singing: "It's the most wonderful time of the year." I totally identify. Back to school.

My kids have come to accept this yearly euphoria of mine, but they can't understand it. For years I've tried to tell them it was due to my excitement over their quest for knowledge and truth, but they don't buy it — especially after finding movie ticket stubs in my pockets and smelling Milk Duds on my breath.

The truth is, after the first week or two — after I've walked the length of the mall a dozen times, after I've written my name with their Etch-a-Sketch and conducted marriages for Barbie and Ken as well as all the stuffed bears and plastic trolls, after I've called everyone I know (and a few people I don't) — I start to miss having them around. (But don't tell them!)

They think they go to school for their education — to learn about line graphs and polar ice caps, about the periodic table of elements and Hester Prynne — and for those things they do. But for their real education — for learning where the salad fork goes and how to make hospital corners on a bed, how to swallow aspirin and the proper way to answer the phone — that's what home is for.

Home is where a child learns about love and commitment, connectedness and belonging, self-control, self-confidence, and coping with disappointment. It's where a child learns about limits and discipline, honor, respect, and integrity. It's where table manners are practiced, traditions passed on, rites of passage celebrated, and roots dug deep. Home is where lives are shaped, charity is practiced, and where values are formed.

Home allows patience and endurance to be tested over and over and over. It's where a child can make wrong choices, fall and fail, then get back up and find forgiveness. It's where a child can grow: body, soul, and spirit.

As a Christian parent, I am responsible for their lessons in holiness and training in godliness, for their basic and advanced studies in ceaseless prayer and uncompromising obedience, in trusting that which cannot be seen and persevering under pressure.

As God teaches me, so I in turn teach my children as we sit at home and when we walk along the road, when we lie down and when we get up (Deuteronomy 6:7).

"So what are you doing wandering around an airport?" someone asked. It wasn't an audible voice that spoke, but it was a voice nonetheless.

I gasped and looked around at the men in suits, the sweeping man, and the reading nun, none of whom appeared to be talking to me.

"Well?"

I looked around again. No one had spoken to me. No one that is, except God.

I gulped and answered, "Doing research? Gathering knowledge? Giving the family a valuable lesson in independence?"

I waited for a reply, but the airport (and God) was silent, except for the usual sounds of passengers bustling about and the instrumental version of Barry Manilow's "Mandy" playing over the sound system.

"I know! I know!" I said. "I'm teaching them that I'm not their slave and that I was not put on this earth to serve them."

Again, silence (except: "Oh, Mandy...you came and you gave without taking...").

One more time I scanned the airport and cocked my ear to listen for the voice, but it had ceased speaking to me. As the quiet thundered throughout my being, I picked up my suitcase and inched it toward the ticket counter. With each tug on the handle, I breathed a prayer that the closer I got to my destination, the closer I'd get to what it was I really wanted.

All I had to do was figure out what that was.

"All your sons will be taught by the LORD, and great will be your children's peace" (Isaiah 54:13).

CHAPTER NINETEEN

The First Shall Be Last, and the Last Shall Get First Dibs

WHAT I REALLY WANTED was time for Me. My needs met, my wants satisfied, my whims and every desire catered to. I wanted freedom from the tyranny of routine. I wanted mystery, danger, and intrigue...and an entire dinner conversation that didn't include a dissertation on tapeworms. I wanted to eat Cheetos in bed and not share them with anybody and spend all my money on highlighting my hair and waxing my legs. I wanted to stick my finger in wet cement and sit in the front row at a Huey Lewis and the News concert.

And never again did I want to hear the word "dibs."

At our house we have an elaborate dibs system that has evolved over the years. For example, an ice hockey game on television takes priority over anything else, even if someone has already called dibs on another show. With the car radio, just saying, "I like that song," is the same as calling dibs. The only exceptions are if someone says they hate it first, if I deem the song morally objectionable, or if it's anything by Huey Lewis and the News. (Huey Lewis takes priority at all times. That's my "dibs.")

We wouldn't have a dibs problem if it weren't for the real problem. The real problem is, everybody wants their own way; everybody wants to win. But when it comes to one television show, one song on the radio, or one last Tootsie Roll Pop, if somebody wins, somebody else loses, which no one wants to do. Being a gracious person, I generously offer to allow others to practice the art of graceful losing, but someone usually calls dibs on that, too.

A few years back, World War III erupted in our kitchen over a certain spoon we call the Granola Eating Spoon. Technically, it's a sugar spoon: short and round, the perfect size for eating cereal, especially granola, because the raisins don't fall off the sides. For some reason, everyone in the family goes ape over this particular spoon. One family member (whom we'll call Spoon Grabber, or S.G. for short) started getting up before anyone else, racing to the kitchen, and upon pulling open the silverware drawer, yelling, "I call dibs on the Granola Eating Spoon!"

It was utterly childish the way S.G. hopped around the house with that stupid spoon. Then the fights would begin:

"You had it yesterday."

"So what — I called dibs."

"Well, I call dibs on it for tomorrow."

"Can't — you can only dib one day at a time."

Finally, the arguing got so fevered we called an emergency family meeting: something reserved for serious family problems.

Barry spoke. "Nancy, enough is enough. You're an adult, and you shouldn't be fighting over a spoon."

I hung my head in shame and mumbled, "You're right. I'm sorry. I won't do it again." Then, with my head still down I added, "But I call dibs on the red bowl."

It all boils down to the whole fair/not fair thing. It's not fair that there's only one Granola Eating Spoon in the drawer and that only one person gets to use it. It's not fair that the M & M people totally disregarded my vote and made blue M & M's. It's not fair that chocolate cake is fattening and broccoli isn't. It's not fair that the older Barry gets, the better he looks, and the older I get...I just look old.

Laura doesn't think it's fair being the youngest because she can't stay up as late as she wants or have the final say on her choice of clothes. She says Alison gets everything her own way.

Alison doesn't think it's fair being the oldest because she has to pay her own car insurance and buy her own clothes and she sometimes has to drive Laura somewhere. She says Laura gets everything her own way.

I'll tell you what's not fair, I thought, as I edged my suitcase through the airport. *It's not fair that I always have to be the one to determine fairness.* Half the time I don't know what's fair and the other half I don't care.

I mean, if two people call dibs on the television at precisely the same exact moment, and if there's only one television, how does one go about deciding who gets it?

If I do eenie meenie, everyone knows when you eenie on number one you moe on number two. Or, if you add "My mother told me to pick the very best one and that is you," and even if you throw in "Y-O-U and that spells you," whoever you end up with, it's still Not Fair.

All that inner debate — not to mention everything else that had happened to me that day — was making me hungry. Looking around for someplace to eat and thinking about food got me thinking about granola, which got me thinking about the Granola Eating Spoon, which got me thinking about dibs again. *Lord, You just don't know what I've gone through*, I fumed.

Or maybe He does. The same problem I have with my kids over the television, Jesus had with his disciples when He caught them arguing over who would be greatest in the kingdom of heaven (they'd been calling dibs on who would sit at the Lord's right hand).

Jesus didn't eenie meenie; He told them that whoever wanted to be first must be the very last, and the servant of all (Mark 9:35). I tried explaining that to the girls one day after a particularly heated dibs match over the last can of Diet Pepsi. I told them the parable of the man who grabbed the best seat at a wedding feast and was embarrassed when the host told him to sit in the least seat and gave his seat to another guest.

After explaining the parable, I drank the soda and sent them outside to pick weeds. Afterwards I further illustrated the parable by setting out one Snickers bar cut in two unequal pieces.

"OK, Laura, you choose which one you want," I said.

She looked at me, looked at Alison, then froze. "This is a trick, isn't it?" she said and refused to even touch the candy.

I turned to Alison. "OK, then. You pick."

She refused also. Then they both grabbed a handful of pretzels and I was left with both pieces of candy bar — which illustrated my point perfectly.

That is, it satisfied my sweet tooth perfectly. I still hadn't gotten my point across. So, I kept offering them unequal choices. I had it planned that whoever took the better one first would find it taken away and given to her sister. But both girls shrewdly turned down my offers of candy, cookies, and even cold, hard cash.

Just when I thought I'd never get my point across, a situation that spoke loudly and clearly presented itself. It was a Sunday morning. We walked into church, and as I started to take my usual place in the front row, I noticed someone had put a Bible on my chair. I couldn't believe it! Obviously it was a mistake, so I removed it and placed it on a seat behind me.

As the service began, one of the deacons approached me and asked if I would sit someplace else; they needed my seat for the guest soloist (who had a sprained ankle) since my seat was the easiest one for her to use.

I felt my face turn red, especially after Laura whispered, "But, Mom, you called dibs!"

After church was over and we were headed to the car, Laura stopped short and slapped her forehead with her palm. "Oh, I get it!" she said. "The candy, the Diet Pepsi, you kicking the lady with the sprained ankle out of her seat — when you get greedy you get stuff taken away, and when you're unselfish you get good stuff. It's like, the first are last, and the last get first dibs."

By jove, I think she's got it.

Now if only I could get it, I thought as I scooted my suitcase toward the airport coffee shop. What I really wanted to "get" was the knowledge of what I really wanted — and to know where on earth I could find it.

I mused. I pondered. I meditated. And then…I realized what I really wanted: A piece of pie.

"For whoever exalts himself will be humbled, and whoever humbles himself will be exalted" (Matthew 23:12).

CHAPTER TWENTY

Give Us This Day Our Daily Bread — But Cut the Crusts Off

IN THE BOOK *Tales of a Fourth Grade Nothing*, a character named Fudge eats a live turtle. Obviously, he's not what you'd call a picky eater. I'm not sure how I'd like to have a turtle-noshing offspring, but at least it would be a welcome relief from having to plan and cook meals around one who doesn't like rice and one who doesn't like potatoes, one who prefers white meat only and one who thinks it's barbaric to eat anything that once had a face.

We have one family member who will only eat a sandwich with the mustard next to the cheese and the mayonnaise next to the lettuce, and one who will eat peanut butter without jelly and jelly without peanut butter, but never peanut butter and jelly together — AND NO CRUSTS!!!

I used to suffer great mental anguish over the problem of what to pack in the girls' school lunches. Crustless hunks of bread I could handle, but having to come up with creative, nutritious, faceless fillings that weren't egg salad ("too stinky") or PB & J (one didn't like it, the other one called it "baby food") I found a bit too taxing at seven o'clock on a school day morning. I used to remind the girls that my mom used to fix us leftover spaghetti or mashed potato sandwiches, but they whined that they'd die of embarrassment if I ever did that to them.

I knew from experience (after all, I was a kid myself once) that apples end up in the trash can, uneaten; bananas get the guts squished out of them first, then end up in the trash can, uneaten; and carrot and celery sticks don't even rate being taken out of the lunch bag at all. The only foods I was ever certain my kids would eat were the factory-packaged, gooey, artificially-colored and flavored, chemical-infested, sugar-and-fat-laden, crunchy munchies. And I never wanted the Food Police or Richard Simmons or a well-meaning cafeteria lady to know I actually feed such stuff to my children.

So what did I end up packing? Well, let's just say, if you are what you eat, my children are boxed apple juice, hunks of crustless bread with globs of cream cheese, and round, flat pieces of dried, pureed, fruit-flavored, rolled-up things you buy in the produce section of the market.

About three years ago I quit packing their school lunches altogether. They'd both reached an age where they were old enough to spell Cheez Whiz and tall enough to reach the Ho Ho's in the pantry. Being the intelligent girls they are, I naturally assumed they'd pack well-balanced, nutritious food, or at least hit one or two of the basic food groups.

Since both girls appear well-nourished, I never questioned them until last year when I noticed Laura's lunch bags were looking rather skimpy. I took a look: a can of Diet Pepsi, a bag of pretzels, five Tootsie Roll Pops, and a kosher dill pickle.

When I asked her about it, she gave me one of those middle-schooler head tilts, put her hands on her hips, and recited the nutritional components of her lunch: the beverage group, the snack group, the vegetable group, and the fruit-flavored group.

Duh.

One of the great challenges of motherhood is raising a family with one or more picky eaters. I know a woman who breaks out in hives when she goes into a fast food restaurant with her three daughters. She orders three cheeseburgers: one without catsup, one without mustard or onions, and one without catsup, mustard, onions, pickles, bun, or meat. What gives her hives is the counter clerk's usual response: "Lady, are you nuts?" (Or something to that effect.) This woman has a child who will only eat cheese, and fast food restaurants won't sell her just a slice of cheese, so she's learned to order cheeseburgers sans everything but the cheese.

I know another woman who has resorted to what some may call trickery, but most moms would call creative thinking. She gives "yucky" foods favorite cartoon character names: Barney Bran Flake Cereal, Big Bird Scrambled Eggs, Oscar the Grouch Asparagus, and Little Mermaid Split Pea Soup.

I tried that once with a casserole I made out of canned corned beef, cream of mushroom soup, spinach, and Velveeta cheese, calling it Popeye Pie. They renamed it Pepe le P.U. This Stinks Over Rice.

For the most part, however, my girls have outgrown their tantrums over microscopic particles of onion in meat loaf and their hissy fits over gravy touching the peas on the plate.

Alison — the one who lost her lunch all over the bathroom door on New Year's Eve 1989 after eating carrot sticks dipped in (spoiled) ranch dressing — is still distrustful of food. She questions everything she puts in her mouth, sniffing it and demanding proof that the expiration date on packages are accurate. Then she still throws out half the food in the refrigerator.

As for Laura, she'll eat anything as long as it rhymes with "eat-za" or can be served out of a drive-through window. Mostly, though, they both like to eat hunks of bread.

As I took a seat in the airport coffee shop and ordered a piece of strawberry rhubarb pie, I couldn't help overhearing a woman giving instructions in table manners to her brood of three young boys. "Now, we're having chicken nuggets and french fries. You will not put your french fries in your nose, your ear, or your drink — or anyone else's nose, ear, or drink. You will not show each other your chewed-up food, and you will not play the 'Want to know what this looks like?' game. You will keep your hands on your own plate, you will not say, 'Look over there,' and steal each other's french fries, and you will not make soda come out your nose. Do you understand, boys?"

I'm not sure the boys understood. But I did.

I used to have similar conversations with my girls. ("Don't stab your bread with your fork. Don't stab your sister with your fork. Don't stab your sister with HER fork. *Give me that fork.* Use your spoon.")

Over the past few years, my biggest concern has been, "Who's going to spill their iced tea first?" *At least I don't have to worry about them asking embarrassing questions,* I reminded myself after overhearing one of the boys ask the waitress, "Aren't you kinda old to have a tooth missing?"

Every table should come with a button that mothers can press to open an escape hatch in the floor. I remember teaching Alison to say, "Bless you," when somebody sneezed. One day when we were in a restaurant, the man at the table behind us let out a booming, "Ahhhhh-CHOOO!" Alison stood up on her seat and popped her head over the booth. "Oh, look, Mommy!" she shouted. "That man got 'bless you' all over his food!"

I laughed at the memory and finished my pie just in time to hear a loud, "Please, Mom? Please, can I have some bread? Just one piece of bread?"

It came from the table of boys — one of them was hanging over his chair and grabbing at the bread basket on the next table while his mother grabbed at the back of his shirt. (With the other hand she frantically searched for the escape hatch button.) Meanwhile, the oldest-looking boy grabbed french fries off the bread-grabber's plate and the youngest one yelled, "This chicky nuggy is gwoss."

"Just one piece of bread!" the boy begged. "Pleeeeeze?"

All eyes were on the boy and his embarrassed mother as she pried his fingers away from the next table, then carried him off to the ladies' room for, as I heard her call it, a "discussion." As I waited for the waitress to bring my check, I thought about the way the boy begged for that bread. In a way, he had the right idea — he just had the wrong bread.

We have a problem at our house with bread. People leave the bags open and it gets stale. Or they'll track crumbs all through the house. Or someone will insist I bought the wrong kind. They're so picky!

One of the jokes in our family is that Barry insists bread in a paper bag tastes different than the same bread in a plastic bag. I go to the bakery every day and ask for a loaf of Italian bread in a paper bag.

"Give me this day my daily bread," I say to the woman behind the counter, and she laughs. If Alison and Laura are with me, they'll roll their eyes and say, "Oh, Mom, you're so lame," or they pretend they don't know me — until we're in the parking lot.

Then they beg me for "just a piece."

Sometimes, as I break off a hunk and hand it to them, I'll remind them: "Unlike this, there's another Bread that never goes stale, who sustains life and who satisfies the deepest hunger."

This is the bread you should beg for, kid, I thought, as the boy and his mother returned to their table. That's what I tell my girls: Grab onto Jesus, the One who calls Himself the Bread of Life, and beg, "Feed me 'til I want no more!"

Crusts and all.

"He who feeds on this bread will live forever" (John 6:58).

CHAPTER TWENTY-ONE

What Happens When Mothers Pray

I CONTINUED WANDERING around the airport, stopping every few feet to set down my suitcase and rub my sore palm on my thighs. Then I'd either grab the handle and drag it or nudge the suitcase along with my foot. After ten minutes or so, I hobbled into the gift shop for a bag of M & M's — brain food — to help me focus on choosing a destination.

I nudged my suitcase over to the row of chairs facing the huge picture window and sat down to watch the planes take off. As I picked out the blue M & M's, I couldn't help envying the people in the planes who knew where they were going. "Flight 326 to Dayton...Flight 74 to Albany...Flight 104 to Oklahoma...now boarding at Gate 61."

Oklahoma! I turned it over in my mind. Where the wind comes whistling down the plains. Surreys with the fringe on top. Oklahoma, O-K. I was just starting to get a glimmer of a mini-spark of a fraction of an idea when a loud, "Jimmy, don't do —" interrupted my thoughts.

I turned around as a woman lunged after a speeding bullet in green overalls who had, by the time she caught him, begun licking the observation window. She grabbed him by his shoulder straps with one hand and dragged him over to the row of seats behind me. At the same time, she stopped his shoe in midair with the other hand as he pulled it off his foot and hurled it through the air.

"Jimmy, Mommy says —"

Jimmy shook his brown mop of curls as hard as he could, broke free of Mommy, and licked the chair next to me. Then he licked my chair.

"I'm so —" Mommy said. "You see, Jimmy, he's, well —"

The poor woman. She'd contracted the dreaded Halfsies Syndrome. That's what happens to a woman once she has small children. As soon as she opens her mouth to speak, whether it be while she's on the phone or as she's attempting a conversation with the grocery cashier, her sentences are immediately cut off by someone wailing, "C'n I hab some joosh?" or an incessant, "Huh, Mom? Huh, Mom? Mom! Mom! Mom!" As a result, mothers tend to talk in half-sentences.

Years ago I attended a church prayer seminar at which everyone was asked to pray in sentence prayers. All the women looked at the leader as if he had told us to speak Swahili. Then someone in the back of the room raised her hand and asked, "What's a —?"

Mommy and I sat down for awhile and halved out a conversation while Jimmy licked everything he could get his tongue on when Mommy (who's name turned out to be Donna) wasn't looking.

Donna shook her own brown curls and sighed. "Did you ever feel like —"

"Getting a perm?" I asked.

"No, running —"

"Away?"

She nodded and wiped off Jimmy's tongue with a tissue after he licked the bottom of his shoe.

"Yeah," I answered (in a complete sentence — there are rare moments of sentence wholeness, especially once your children get older). "That's what I'm doing!"

She gathered up the socks Jimmy had pulled off and thrown on the floor, retrieved his shoes from a trash can, and smiled at me. "Maybe someday I can join —"

I returned the smile and watched her chase after her barefoot toddler. With her few, short half-sentences she'd convinced me I was doing the right thing. I owed it to all mothers of curl shakers and shoe lickers across America to go through with it. I was a role model, a heroine of sorts. Maybe they'd put my picture on a stamp. Or a silver coin. I'd be right up there with Susan B. Anthony and Harriet Tubman and Amelia Earhart. Maybe they'd even make a movie of my life (starring Meg Ryan as the perky, yet thoughtful and brave runaway mom).

My running away would be a symbol of strength and courage. I was doing this for the entire sisterhood of mothers. Doing it in response to grape juice stains on the drapes, drains clogged with modeling clay, and dirty underwear stuffed way in the backs of dresser drawers everywhere.

With renewed purpose and energy, I took a deep breath and picked up my suitcase. I marched to the front of the ticket line, slammed my fist on the counter, and shouted, "OK, Blake. I'm ready to roll!"

Blake clicked his pen, rolled up his shirt sleeves, and grinned. "OK. Let 'er rip. Where did you decide you're going?"

I looked him in the eye and said, "Somewhere where a mom can carry on a conversation without having to stop mid-sentence and shout, 'I told you NOT TO USE YOUR SHOES TO CARRY DIRT — THAT'S WHAT YOUR BUCKET IS FOR!' or say, 'We'll discuss whether or not your sister's a puke head when I'm off the phone.' I want to go somewhere where a twelve-pack of Diet Pepsi lasts at least two days. Where, when I say something inaccurate or even stupid, I'm not met with a slack-jawed teenager saying, 'Duh.' I want to go where God is and where His glory dwells."

Blake clicked his pen a few times and looked at his computer screen. "I'm sorry, Mrs. K, but I don't see such a place on my monitor." He punched a few buttons and shook his head. "Maybe if you tell me more, I could get a better idea how to help you."

I reviewed my criteria: it had to be a place that I could spell, where I didn't have to wear a bathing suit or learn a new language, and where I could be loved, respected, revered, adored, admired, and appreciated. And costing under $200.

Blake studied his monitor one more time. "How 'bout Cincinnati?" he suggested.

I furrowed my brow and ran my finger through my hair like I always do when I'm trying to concentrate. "C-I-N — nope. Can't spell it. What else you got?"

"Well, there's always Truth or Consequences, New Mexico. You know — New Mexico: The Land of Enchantment?'"

I mulled it over. It did sound enchanting, but writing that return address on an envelope could cause severe writer's cramp.

Earlier I'd thought about Oklahoma, but I remembered Oklahoma was called the Dust Bowl in the 1930s, and I wanted to get away from dust...not run to it.

By this time Blake's smile had started to fade. That's when I knew I'd hit a wall. Finally, I gave up. "This is *not* working," I told him and stepped away from the counter. "It's no use. There's nothing more I can do."

I walked away, dragging my suitcase and bemoaning the fact that I'd never be a heroic role model if I couldn't choose a destination. Then an errant thought struck me.

I could pray about it.

What a novel idea. A former pastor's wife always used to say, "God can't answer what you don't ask." She was also fond of saying, "You never know what happens when mothers pray."

One more time, my suitcase and I found a seat, and I prepared myself to pray. Normally I did most of my praying scrunched up in odd positions, such as when I'm bending over to make the bed or with my head in the oven trying to clean the back wall. Sometimes I pray with outstretched arms while dusting ceiling fans, sometimes prostrate on the ground trying to fish something out from under the couch. Usually I pray on the run, sometimes in frantic bursts of desperation. This time, though, I actually sat down.

What happens when mothers pray? I'll never forget the time I got together with my friend, Marian. We both had toddlers and both wanted to spend some time in prayer together, but had always found it impossible to do.

One day we set our minds to DO IT. We prayed before we prayed, "Lord, please send an angel to occupy Laura and Essie so we can spend this time together with You."

God answered our prayer, but He must've sent an angel of mischief. After about half an hour of wonderful, deep prayer time, we noticed the house was quiet. Too quiet. And we were scared. Any mother knows that two two-year-olds plus one too quiet house equals trouble.

In walked our mischief makers, giggling and with blue stripes down their tongues. They'd gotten into a carton of Christmas ornaments, had taken the ones painted with tempera — licked them — then dragged them all (dozens of them!) into the bathroom and washed them one by one. Not only that, the paint they couldn't get off with water had been wiped off with the contents of Marian's linen closet.

THAT'S what happens when mothers pray!

When mothers pray, things happen. When they pray for patience, their kids come down with chicken pox. When mothers pray for character, they're given a child of like temperament who acts as the sandpaper God uses to refine their rough edges.

When mothers pray for endurance and energy, their children join Little League and Youth Soccer and Children's Choir, all requiring mothers to go farther, harder, longer.

When mothers pray to be made more like Jesus, they receive a lifetime of opportunities to serve and suffer and die to themselves.

What happens when mothers pray? Grace is poured down from heaven's window, faith is rewarded, peace reigns in hearts, joy overflows, and children are brought into the kingdom of God.

Yeah, but will praying help me find my direction? I wondered as I began to pray:

"Father in heaven, I'm tired. My car smells like a deli. They broke the jar of mustard. I don't know where to go. I don't know what to do. You've brought me this far, and I know You'll lead me to where you want me.... I just hope it's not one of those Caribbean islands that always get swept away by hurricanes or anyplace too cold in the winter.

"Lord, I want to go where my gifts and talents can be used and where my unread magazines don't get cut up until I've had a chance to read them. If it's not too much trouble, I'd like to go where people tighten the pickle jar lids when they put them back in the refrigerator. I want to go where Your glory dwells, where You make Your presence known and where my soul and my spirit can flourish just as You intended. Amen."

After my amen, I gathered up my things quickly (in case that voice inside my head decided to return and further confound my plans). It was time for action. I picked up my suitcase for what I hoped would be the last time, and as I walked up to the ticket counter I remembered the verse in Isaiah that says, "Whether you turn to the right or to the left, your ears will hear a voice behind you, saying, 'This is the way; walk in it'" (Isaiah 30:21).

I turned my head to the right, to the left...and then I heard it. Behind me, a man in a cowboy hat and snakeskin boots began to sing in a deep voice: "Houston, Houston Oilers...."

"The earnest prayer of a righteous man has great power and wonderful results" (James 5:16 LB).

CHAPTER TWENTY-TWO

Happy Mudder's Day

HOUSTON! LAND OF the free and home of the brave, or something like that. Why hadn't I thought about it earlier? No blizzards in the winter, H-O-U-S-T-O-N...and I was sure there were lots of other good things about the place. Actually, I never really ever wanted to go to Texas, but at that point, I was just relieved that I'd made a decision. Besides, hadn't I heard the voice behind me?

I fairly flew up to the ticket counter singing, "Houston, Houston Oilers, *la la la la la la.*" (I didn't know the rest of the words to the song.) I *la la*-ed away my time in line, hopping from one foot to the other in eager anticipation. When my turn finally came, I grabbed Blake's pen out of his hand, gave it a few clicks, handed it back to him and blurted out, "I want to go to Houston! Home of the Oilers and the Astros and probably other stuff."

I continued my *la la*'s as Blake scanned his monitor.

"Well, Mrs. Kennedy," he said after my third round of *La la la la la la,* "you're in luck. We have a flight to Houston leaving at 1:35."

I handed him over my $199 plus tax and sighed. *This is it.* As

I turned to leave, Blake tapped me on the shoulder.

"Mrs. Kennedy, I want to thank you. You remind me so much of my mom, and all day I've been thinking about her. To tell you the truth, I don't talk to her as often as I should. Right after my shift, I'm going to give her a call."

His eyes lit up as he clicked his pen and grinned. "Maybe I'll even send her some flowers — sort of an early Mother's Day present."

It was my turn to grin as I thanked Blake for all his helpful assistance. Then, tucking my ticket inside my purse, I took a seat to wait for my flight to freedom.

I glanced over at Blake — still smiling, still clicking his pen — and thought, *What a nice son to get his mom an early Mother's Day present.*

As for me, I never get what I really want for Mother's Day. Every year the girls ask me, "What do you want?" and every year I give them the same answer: "I want you to make your bed every day, keep your room clean, and be nice to your sister."

To that they reply, "No, really. What do you really want?" Then they buy me a coffee mug or a candle, or they bring me a plant (and take bets on how long it will last until I kill it).

One year Alison gave me lunch — a plate of rice cakes and grape jelly — and a five dollar bill. They say, "What goes around, comes around," and it's true, at least in my case. When it comes to holidays, Martha Stewart I'm not. I mean well, and I have good intentions. I just get sidetracked easily and forget about details until it's too late.

I forget things like tape for wrapping gifts, the grass that goes inside an Easter basket, and the fact that a frozen turkey takes at least three days to thaw out.

I'm not a total lost cause, however. One Easter I actually bought Easter grass *and* baskets *and* candy and other stuff to go in them — I just never got around to making them up. On Easter morning, I handed each of the girls a basket (with the price tags still on) and a bag of green grass, then dumped a pile of candy on the dining room table and said, "Go for it!" I told them it was our new family tradition: do-it-yourself holiday fun. (Now that I think of it, that was just a month before the rice cakes and money for Mother's Day episode.)

Which brings me back to the subject of Mother's Day. My theory is, mothers never get what they really want. My mom always asked for a shower cap, which she never got; my grandmother always asked for a wallet, which she never got either.

Out of curiosity, and with time to kill before my flight to Houston, I polled several women sitting near me. I asked them,

"What do you really want for Mother's Day?"

One woman stared blankly and said, "An entire day without hearing, "Buy me, drive me, fix me, get me, give me."

Another one laughed and said, "To have somebody else put the toilet paper on the roll."

The last woman I asked introduced herself as Julia and launched into her description of a fantasy weekend getaway with her husband.

"Picture this," she said, "you're knee-deep in laundry and overwhelmed by stacks of gravy-encrusted dishes and yellow, waxy build-up on your floors. As you're wondering, *Is this all there is to life?* the doorbell rings. You run to answer it, hoping for...you don't know what, but something. Anything.

"You open the door and gasp: 'Is it really you?' You can barely get the words out to the figure on your doorstep. The bun-haired one smiles. It is Alice, your Brady Bunch fantasy come true, your blue-uniformed answer to prayer."

Julia tilted her head back, closed her eyes, and continued.

"While you gush and fawn and prostrate yourself on the floor, Alice dusts off your doorknob, steps inside, and announces you are the winner of a Mother's Day dream vacation. As part of the grand prize package, she's there to stay with the children, scour the pink slime out of your shower, and stock your kitchen with gourmet delights.

"After a quick search for strings attached (and a sigh of relief at not finding any), you tiptoe (lest this be a dream) into your bedroom, where you discover that not only is your closet jammed with romantic floral sun dresses, white cotton sweaters without baby spit up on the shoulder, and size eight jeans, but you now have a body that fits into all of them."

As Julia talked, she attracted a crowd of women, all with fantasy ideas of their own. Picking up the story, someone added, "A car horn beeps from the driveway, drawing your attention away from the closet. Wearing his bicep-revealing black shirt, your husband awaits in a red '67 Mustang, white-top convertible, with Johnny Mathis serenading "Chances Are" on the radio. You run outside, toss your luggage in the back seat, and together you speed off toward your ideal vacation spot.

"'Shall we discuss our innermost thoughts and dreams for the future?' your husband asks, his brown eyes intent on your own baby blues.

"'What, no talk of the upcoming weed and feed lawn treatment?' you answer. 'No boring hockey stats? No burping to the tune of "La Bamba?"'

"'This is your dream vacation,' he says, taking your hand.

'Only witty, Spencer Tracy–Katherine Hepburn style repartee allowed. No burping, no nose-blowing, no talk of mulching in the spring.'"

Yet another woman continued, "Confused but delighted, you toss your hair in the wind as you drive along, discussing Deep Subjects interspersed with playful banter à la any Woody Allen movie. You head for — as the brochure in your hand describes — a secluded romantic hideaway, a nineteenth-century reminder of a less-hurried time.

"The sun sets just beyond your destination: a custard-yellow Victorian bed and breakfast inn. The scent of roses and gardenias greets you as you stroll arm in arm through a vine-covered arbor and up a winding staircase to your corner room, overlooking an English garden."

At this point, everyone stopped to imagine the scene. Then Julia (who started the whole thing originally) continued. "You light an array of candles which casts an amber glow over the room. Faint strains from a string quartet downstairs add to the ambiance and fuel your anticipation. As you climb into the carved oak bed and draw back the English rose quilt, your cream-colored satin lingerie slides across your tanned legs. Outside the window, a gentle rain begins to fall. Except for the soft music, all is quiet."

By that time, we'd attracted a few others who joined us in a chorus of *ooh-la-las* and giggles. Then I picked up the story.

"With the lingering scent of lime shaving cream and Old Spice on his face, your husband joins you. Alone at last, your attention draws to thoughts of your deepest desires: wolfing down bags of Cool Ranch Doritos and peanut butter M & Ms, chugging orange juice from the carton, and playing Tetris on your daughter's Game Boy until way past your bedtime.

"You wolf, you chug, you stay up until 9:15. You enter paradise. In the morning, nobody jumps on your stomachs or puts their finger in your ears to jolt you awake. Instead, the aroma of french roasted coffee and something other than cold cereal or leftover pizza gently nudges you out of bed for yet another round of Tetris."

This brought a round of laughs, and Julia finished with, "You ask yourself, *Will this madcap vacation never end?* as you spend the next twenty-four hours NOT changing diapers, NOT refereeing fights over whose turn it is to sit in the front seat, and NOT getting just one more bedtime drink of water. You wear clothes without miniature jellied hand prints on them and eat in restaurants that serve food not prefaced by Mc.

"When you arrive home, the children play quietly together, your suitcases magically unpack themselves, and a candlelight dinner awaits you."

Julia took a breath and sighed. "But in the real world, just as Alice announces her decision to leave the Bradys and stay on with your family permanently, someone jumps on your stomach, or a child's finger pokes at your ear, and a tray of soggy toast and cold coffee shoved under your nose startles you out of your dream.

"'Time to wake up, Mommy,' a voice calls in your ear. 'Happy Mudder's Day.'"

With that, fantasy time ended, and the women all went back to what they'd come to the airport to do. Since I still had time before my flight, I took the opportunity to pray for Julia, who had excused herself to take her seven-year-old son to the bathroom. She had seemed burdened and worn, and my heart ached for her.

I prayed for this dear woman who wondered, "Is this all there is to life?" and who seemed overwhelmed by the mundane tasks that make up her day. "Lord, let her know that as she continually spills out her life for her young ones, whether by tying shoelaces or wiping backsides and noses, that her reward will be worth the effort. Show her that every day, Jesus will provide strength for her tasks, eternal purpose for her life, endless grace to continue, and the complete satisfaction of knowing her work in the Lord is never in vain. Amen."

I breathed a sigh of contentment. I'd done my good deed, I'd prayed for a sister, and now I was about to embark on a new adventure.

My mind was set on Houston.

"Her children arise and call her blessed" (Proverbs 31:28).

CHAPTER TWENTY THREE

Ask Me No Questions...and I'll Be Eternally Grateful

I CHECKED IN my suitcase and wandered through the airport looking for my boarding gate. Up to this point, I'd been concentrating on making my escape. But now that I was on my way, the hard questions began. *Now what? I've decided to go to Houston, but what will I do when I get there? How long should I stay? Will my family miss me? When I go home, will things be the same as when I left? Will the mustard situation change? Will there still be footprints on the wall?*

What if when I get home, my family still doesn't wipe strawberry jam off the garage wall when the jar misses the trash can? What if they still play tug of war with the remote control and step over the shoes left in the front entryway?

How will they survive while I'm gone? Will the soap in the shower ever find its way up off the floor and onto the soap dish? Will anybody notice if it doesn't? Will anybody care if I'm not there to see that it's done?

Question, questions. I didn't know what to do...I didn't even know the whereabouts of my boarding gate. I had all the questions; I just didn't know The Answer. Not only that, my questions were about to drive me crazy.

Can I survive a month or even a week on my own? What if I can't sleep without my feather pillow that has taken twenty years to break in just right? Who will cut my hair the way I like it? Who will laugh at my jokes? Who will make me laugh?

Standing in the middle of the airport concourse, the irony of my situation struck me, and I started laughing. Not your gentle, ladylike twitter, but your full-scale, hyena-like laugh that generally causes people to point and stare. There I was, running away from, among other things, nineteen years' worth of incessant questions that I knew would eventually sizzle my brain like cooked eggs, and it was my own questions that were about to send me frying.

You know how it is. You think it's so incredibly cute when your little one asks, "Who made my nose? Who made my feet? Who made the dog's feet?" You even think it's unbelievably adorable when that same little one asks, "Does God have a beard?" and "Did Jesus eat hot dogs?" You may even think it's enormously enchanting when that child asks his grandfather, "Grandpa, if man was made in God's image, does that mean he has hair in his ears like you do?"

However, no matter how you do the math, cute, adorable, enchanting questions twelve thousand times a day times nineteen years equals fried eggs for brains.

My personal least favorites include the entire Why series and all its derivatives ("Why is the grass green? Why do I have five fingers? Why don't cows meow? Why can't I go downtown and play Silly String cars with all my friends and stay out until after midnight? Why does your head look like it's going to fly off into outer space any minute?").

Tied with the Why series is the silly, mindless, endless What Ifs that are popular with five- and six-year-olds ("What if this bowl of cereal was really dog food and when people ate it they turned into dogs, and then what if the dogs all got together and they all turned into pianos? What if the ocean was made out of grape Kool-Aid and birds drove tractor trailers and ate bologna sandwiches? What if you rode a toilet to school and your name was Burp Burp?")

A sub-category of the endless What Ifs are the older child's version of Hypothetically Speaking, of which Laura reigns as Hypothetical Queen. These questions usually involve a potentially important (i.e., costly) piece of information wrapped in an innocent-sounding query. For example: "Hypothetically speaking, what happens to carpeting when red food coloring is spilled on it?" or, "Hypothetically speaking, what would happen if someone accidentally put pork chop bones down the garbage disposal, and how much would it cost to fix it?"

I thought I'd reached my limit shortly after the hypothetical pork chop incident (which, for further hypothetical information, costs $157.39 to fix). I called my mom and asked her, "Mom, do kids' questions ever go away? Do they ever stop? Is there any documented evidence of a woman's head exploding after listening to eight straight hours of, 'Why does Mickey Mouse have only four fingers?' and 'Why do people have earlobes?' Do they ever stop, Mom? Do they, huh? And what if...."

Mom laughed and told me, "No, the questions never stop; in fact, they get harder to answer."

She got that one right. They go from pointing to your nose and asking, "What zat?" to "How do I know if the Bible is true?" and "Is it really so wrong to have sex before marriage if the entire culture says it's right?" And in between they ask about earlobes and nose hair and why mommies shave under their arms and daddies don't.

Questions, questions. I'm constantly amazed that my kids think I know all the answers ("Mom, what exactly is thermodynamics, and how does it apply to my life?"). Just the other day Alison popped her head out of her room and asked, "Quick — Mom, what's an African animal that eats its young?"

The problem is, I know the answers, but they just don't ask the right questions.

I know that Albert Einstein's brain is stored in a Mason jar in Wichita, Kansas, and that it takes sixty chinchillas to make a chinchilla coat. I also know that the thing used to measure your feet in a shoe store is called a Brannock device. Of course, the most obvious response to that information is, "Who cares?" but that's not the point. The point is: I'm a font of trivia tidbits, but normally no one bothers to ask me about such bits of tid and they seldom come up in everyday conversation. As a result, the girls' questions are usually met with a shrug of my shoulders and an "I don't know — go look it up."

I have questions of my own. Did Adam and Eve have belly buttons? What do babies dream about? Is ear hair God's design or a result of sin? What ever happened to Charles Benson, and how can I thank him for telling me about Jesus way back in junior high school?

As a mother, I've wrestled with questions over movies that everybody else's mom says are OK and whether or not a sixth grader is old enough for an after-school dance. How do I know if I'm doing the right thing? How can I tell if I'm too strict or too lenient? What if my child chooses the wrong path in life? Can I stop her? Can I change her? Is it my fault?

Where's the line between helping a child and trying to live her life for her? Can a mother shoulder all her child's burdens? Should she? If not, how can she let go?

I've never gone to journalism school, but I do know that the cardinal rule for reporters is to go directly to the source with your questions.

God may not answer all my questions, and I'll probably have to wait until I get to heaven to find the answer about Adam and Eve's anatomy and the whereabouts of Charles Benson. But like a good parent, He'll tell me everything I need to know.

All I have to do is ask.

"Ask and it will be given to you; seek and you will find; knock and the door will be opened to you" (Luke 11:9).

I Get By with a Little Help from My Friends

EVENTUALLY I FOUND the correct boarding gate. There, my attention was captured by a drama involving two older women who whispered to one other while pointing toward a younger woman with a baby in a stroller. They shook their heads and clicked their tongues, then approached her. From across the room I smiled. I knew exactly what the pair were going to say, and sure enough they did: "That baby needs a hat."

I think every stroller should come equipped with a sign that says, "Thank you for your concern, but my baby is just fine." I could tell by that young mother's face that she wished she had one as she forced a smile, nodded, and thanked the woman for bringing her negligence to her attention.

The irony is, if your baby is wearing a hat someone will tell you, "It's much too warm for a hat; that baby's going to roast to death." But the minute you remove it, someone else will approach you, wag her finger in your face, and make you feel like you've committed the unpardonable sin.

It starts before your baby is even born. Strangers come up to you in the market and say things like, "You wouldn't have all that awful water retention if you ate lemon rinds and drank hot sauerkraut juice," or "You're so big, you must be having a boy." They'll warn you not to eat whatever it is in your shopping cart and actually return it to the shelves, replacing it with instant tapioca pudding and canned Swiss chard.

One time, during my seventh or eighth month of pregnancy with Laura, I was minding my own business slurping on a Slurpee outside of a Seven Eleven when I was accosted by a tongue-tsking elderly woman. "Why aren't you wearing a sweater?" she demanded. "That baby's going to catch its death of cold! What kind of a mother doesn't keep her baby warm?"

I immediately apologized to her, went right home, and put on a sweater — and a hat. That it was the middle of June and in the upper eighties didn't occur to me as I sweated in the middle of my living room the rest of the day. I'd been duped by an old wives' tale, or at least by an old wife.

As I watched the young mother tie a hat onto her baby's head — then remove it when the women walked away — I laughed. *Good for you*, I thought.

I've received my share of advice over the years: some good, some not so good. Good advice: Never feed your child huge quantities of dried prunes. Don't go to the ladies' room just as they're about to vote for the PTA fund-raiser chairman. If your child is looking a little green and says she's not hungry, don't tell her to eat "one last bite for Mommy."

Not so good advice: Chicken pox isn't contagious until

AFTER the spots break out. Feed your child BEFORE letting her ride the Gravitron at the fair. You'll look better as a blonde.

I've also given my share of bad advice: Just look at Alison's third-grade school picture and ask her why she's wearing a droopy lace bow in her hair.

It seems everybody has an opinion about everything. However, I've just about given up offering mine, especially to the girls — they never take my advice anyway.

I'd be flattered the girls ask my opinion about anything, except I know it's a trap. They don't really want my opinion; they just like to see my eyes roll back in my head and watch me hyperventilate as they shoot down my every "Wear the blue one" with a counterattack of "The blue one? Oh, gross!"

Here's a typical shoe-shopping expedition: We're in the store. Daughter X holds up two pairs of sneakers and asks, "Mom, which do you like better?"

I answer, "I like them both."

"Pick one," she insists.

"OK, I like the white ones."

She bursts into tears. "What's wrong with the black ones?"

Staving off my own tears, I reply, "Nothing's wrong with them. I said I liked them."

"No you didn't. You said they'll make my feet look ugly."

Sensing this is a losing battle, I tell her, "So get the black ones."

To that she responds, "Why can't I get the white ones?"

"Get the white ones then."

She then tilts her head and says, "I don't know. You pick."

Here's another ironic observation: They ask my advice, I give it, they reject it. They get on the phone to a friend, ask that friend for her advice, THAT FRIEND GIVES THE SAME ANSWER I'VE

JUST GIVEN, and they not only accept it, they love it.

"Thank you, thank you, thank you!" they shout into the phone. "You're a lifesaver! How could I live without you?"

Meanwhile, I'm checking myself to see if I've turned invisible.

The Hat Patrol moved on as the Stroller Woman welcomed a young man who had arrived on a flight from Atlanta. Then the Moment I'd been waiting for arrived as a woman's voice announced over the loudspeaker: "Flight number thirty-seven to Houston now boarding at gate sixty-five."

There's no turning back now. My heart raced and my stomach churned as I made my way through the carpet-lined tunnel. On the way to my seat, I grabbed an extra complimentary airline barf bag "just in case."

As I buckled myself into my seat, my thoughts continued to spin. Was I doing the right thing? Would my family be all right? Should I *really* have taken the remote control?

After a few minutes, however, the plane began to taxi down the runway. As the plane began to soar, so did my mood, and I let myself give in to feelings of excitement.

I can't believe I'm doing this! I smiled as I thought about all the times my friends and I had talked about running away. *I can't wait to tell Mary Ann....*

That's when I realized that Mary Ann was back in Florida and I was on my way to Houston.

Hoping to distract myself from my feelings of disappointment, I put on the headphones the flight attendant had given me and flipped through the channels, landing on a Samba version of "I Get By with a Little Help from My Friends." A pang of nostalgia tugged at my heart. There's nothing like having a friend to share things with: stories, laughter, wisdom, advice....

My thoughts switched to the Hat Patrol back at the airport, and I chuckled. *I wonder what advice they'd have for me.* I rested my head on my seat back and smiled as I recalled some of the advice given to me by friends over the years: Don't wear horizontal stripes. Buy food in bulk. Dump the blue eye shadow.

Bonnie told me to hang in there and not give up during a hard time in my marriage. Mary Ann told me to pray over every corner in my house during that same time. Becky kept reminding me, "This is a wonderful opportunity to trust the Lord!"

The best advice I've ever received has been through the quiet witness of friends' lives. Tom has leukemia and last year a bone marrow transplant failed. He's lost his hair but not his sense of humor or his optimism, and he's not afraid to die. He says, "What's the worst that could happen to me? I could go to heaven and see Jesus? That would be the best that could happen!"

Ted and Betty have been married over fifty years. They only have eyes for each other and they guard their marriage with vigilance. They guard mine, too, by lifting Barry and me up to the Father in prayer.

Karen struggles to make ends meet, yet her attitude is always, "I have enough for today; I don't need to worry about tomorrow."

Friends prop us up when we falter and rejoice with us when we soar. They tell us when we err and hold us accountable. They hear our confessions and keep our darkest secrets — and love us in spite of sin. Friends complement our weaknesses, and together we are strong.

And when friends tell you, "That baby needs a hat," they do it out of love.

"A friend loves at all times, and a brother is born for adversity" (Proverbs 17:17).

CHAPTER TWENTY-FIVE

The Flight to Serendipity

THROUGHOUT THE FIRST leg of my journey, I reminisced about adventures I'd had with various friends. I was just thinking about the time Terry and I ran out of gas and ended up hitching a ride with a woman driving a van with a pig in her passenger seat, when the pilot announced our arrival in Atlanta, where I would change planes.

I looked at my watch. Three o'clock. I had an hour to kill before my next flight. *Three o'clock*, I mused as I entered the Atlanta airport. *Laura's probably on the bus, and Alison's probably at the library....*

My thoughts were interrupted by a ruckus not too far from where I sat, as a woman — fortyish, shortish, a tad big-hippish — huffed and puffed past me, wearing an "I've had it" look on her face.

I took a seat in the waiting area, and the woman soon flopped down next to me. After a bit more huffing and puffing on her part, she turned to me and shook her short, auburn hair. With steam coming out of her ears, she blurted out: "They shaved a tennis ball with my new electric razor." Her gray eyes narrowed, the steam increasing with each word. "They snort milk out their noses — on cue. They stuff entire pork chops and whole baked potatoes into their mouths and ask if you like sea food, then open their mouths and say, "See? Food!" They laugh at the word "toilet" and make flushing sounds at the dinner table when they don't like something I've fixed."

She paused and took a breath, then continued: "Yesterday, my ten-year-old, Ryan, took a box of sparklers left over from the Fourth of July and set ants on fire out on the patio, and my older son, Mark, came home from a friend's house with "Go Oilers" shaved in the back of his hair."

I shook my head along with her, a tiny puff of steam starting to come out my own ears. "I know what you mean. But you think boys are bad — you should try having girls. They brush their hair in the kitchen, in the car, in school, in church, in the store. They take hour-long, two-hundred-degree showers and leave razors on the shower floor and Band-Aid wrappers on the sink."

As we waved away the steam emitting from our ears, the woman continued. "Razors? My fifteen-year-old, Mark? One chin whisker — I have more than he does — and he's locked in the bathroom for an hour and a half, the steam from the running water peeling the wallpaper. He comes out with a dozen pieces of toilet paper hanging from his cheeks and four disposable razors tossed in the toilet. He says, 'They're disposable, aren't they?'"

She drew a breath. "You wanna hear about Band-Aids? They put them on the dog's eyebrows. They put them on their shoes. When they run out of duct tape, they use Band-Aids to catch bugs. They cover softballs with them. They leave used ones by the kitchen phone or stuffed in the junk drawer."

I shuddered and changed the subject. "Where are you headed?"

"Orlando," she answered. "I left this morning and took the first flight I could find."

"You just ran away?" I asked. I was incredulous — until I remembered I was doing the very same thing. Then I grinned.

"Hey! Me, too! Only I'm running *from* Orlando!" We smiled at each other, soulsisters and fellow fugitives from the family.

She introduced herself as Carrie. "I couldn't take it any longer," she said. "Do you know what I got for Mother's Day last year? The boys and my husband chipped in to buy me a seven hundred dollars 'home maintenance system.' Anyway you look at it, it's a vacuum cleaner. They bought me a vacuum cleaner." She pursed her lips and growled.

"Oooh, you poor thing!" I told her. "But that's nothing. One year my girls got me a bunch of clothes that ended up in their closets. Another year they made pancakes and dribbled batter all over the carpet — they were mixing it in the hallway — then used a bedspread to clean it up. And you think a vacuum cleaner is bad — my husband got me jumper cables for Christmas."

We continued to shake our heads and alternate grievances against our families. Finally, Carrie said, "My sons cut off all my red American Beauty roses!"

I was about to say, "That's nothing; Laura once washed my car with the back window rolled down," but instead I stopped short. "Why did they do that?" I asked.

Carrie shrugged, then kicked at the carry-on bag at her feet. "Well, they brought them in the house and gave them to me to apologize for denting my car with a golf ball they were rolling off the roof."

"Hunh." I gave my oversized purse a kick, too. "If you ask me, that sounds kinda sweet. Sort of. Like the time Alison taped an 'I Love You, Mom' sign over the hole in her wall after she knocked her baton through it." We both kicked at our bags and smiled at our memories. Sort of.

"I just can't take it anymore," confided my new *compadre*. "I can't."

"Yeah. Me, either," I said.

Carrie thought for a moment, then asked, "Assuming this is your first time, how'd you manage to wait twenty years to run away?"

I laughed and shrugged my shoulders. "I've been gone since early this morning. All day, I've been reliving the past twenty years, and the only thing I know for certain is that if it hadn't been for God's power in my life, I wouldn't have made it this far." I paused. "What about you?" I asked. "Is this your first time?"

She smiled and nodded. "But that doesn't mean I haven't thought about it before." She turned to face me, her eyes intent on mine. "I know what you mean about God. There have been plenty of times when I'd see my boys fighting over the TV remote control or catch them socking each other in the arm — or maybe I'd be in the car and realize I spend a minimum of three hours each day chauffeuring a half-dozen fifth graders around town — and I'd think: *I don't need this. I can't do it.* But…I've done it."

She reached down and pulled a worn, pink Bible out of her bag. "Look here," she said and flipped through the pages. "My favorite verse is in Isaiah where it says God tends His flock like a shepherd, that He gathers the lambs in His arms and carries them close to His heart. Here it is. Isaiah chapter forty, verse eleven." She read aloud: "'He gently leads those that have young.' Right after

Mark was born I wrote in the margin, 'That means mommies!'"
She showed me, then closed the pages and returned her gaze to
the window.

"What I can't understand is, when did God stop gently leading?" she asked, her eyes filling with tears. "The Bible says He gives
strength to the weary and increases the power of the weak, but I'm
so tired. Why did He stop giving it to me?"

My eyes also filled with tears. I'd thought that earlier, too. I'd
thought God had played a practical joke on me. What other reason could there be for toddlers who toss shoes out the car window
while on the freeway, or teenagers who seemingly aim for the mail-
boxes on the side of the road when you're teaching them to drive?
Why bottle caps down the garbage disposal and footprints up
closet walls? Why salt mixed in the sugar bowl and empty ice
cube trays left in the freezer? Why grape jelly on the door knobs?
Why tantrums in the market?

There we sat — two moms on the run — staring out the observation window, sniffing and wiping at our tears, and sorting out all
the reasons we should or should not go home. I still hadn't found
the place where Glory dwelled — not that I believed it was Houston, but I had thought it might be a start.

I looked at my watch again, and my stomach started to knot
up. I wasn't sure if I wanted to continue anymore.

"Carrie, when things get hectic and everybody is accusing
everybody else of making their lives utterly miserable, do you ever
ask yourself, 'What's wrong with this family, and why doesn't God
do something?'"

"All the time," she answered.

"Well, I wonder.... Maybe God is doing something. Not too
long ago, I read in the sixty-eighth Psalm that 'God sets the lonely

in families.' That means families just like mine — and yours."

Apparently, what this meant is that in order for us to be more like Jesus, our family needed a dad who fixes furnaces and who doesn't go to church with us as often as we'd like, one daughter with a mane of dark curls who loves ice hockey and eating pretzels with mustard, another daughter who talks on the phone with her feet on the wall, and a mom who needed to run away in order to find something, only to realize home is the place she'd had it all along.

Carrie nodded. "I always tell the boys, 'Everything God does, He does for a reason, and it's always for His glory and our ultimate good.'" She laughed. "You mean, there's nothing wrong with our families? That, as much as we drive each other crazy, as motley a bunch of misfits as we are, we're hand-picked by God to live together? Oh, wait 'til I tell my husband!"

I thought about home and gave my purse another kick. I thought about the girls. Surprisingly, even one of their fights over hair scrunchies sounded good just then. I wondered if Carrie was missing her family, too.

"Where's your family?" I asked her, "Where are you from?"

She pulled a Rockets cap out of her bag and placed it on her head. "Houston," she said, tapping the brim.

My mouth fell open. "No way!" I cried. I grabbed my fellow runaway's arm. "Carrie, I know this sounds crazy, but I have a ticket to Houston that I'll trade you for your ticket to Orlando."

Carrie looked at me much the same way Barry does when I tell him I made a one-hundred-dollar error in the checkbook — in our favor. "Houston?" she squeaked. "You really have a ticket to Houston? And you want to go to Orlando?"

"Uh-huh," I answered. "That's where I'm from. And to tell you the truth, I don't want to go to Texas anymore. I want to go home!"

She shook her head in disbelief, and as we exchanged tickets, her eyes once again filled with tears. "Me, too," she said.

We quickly gathered up our things, exchanged addresses, and agreed to collect and return each other's suitcases. As I turned to go, Carrie touched my arm. "Nancy, do you know what serendipity is?" she asked.

"Yeah, I think the girls have a bottle of it in the shower — a detangler or something."

She laughed. "No, serendipity's an accidental, fortunate discovery. Meeting you has been serendipitous."

It was my turn to laugh. "Well, Carrie, it's been serendipitous meeting you, too," I said and waved good-bye as she headed for her gate. "Serendipity, huh?" I said as I picked up my suitcase one last time.

"We'll see how serendipitous things are when I get home."

"A man's steps are directed by the LORD" (Proverbs 20:24).

CHAPTER TWENTY-SIX

The Place Where Glory Dwells

THE FUNNY THING about running away is, the place you run from is usually the place you want most to be once you've left...or so I thought until I had found my seat and was headed for home. That's when I remembered the broken dining room chair. And that's when I thought one last time about heading to Mexico or Chicago instead of going home.

You see, the chair broke earlier in the week because certain inhabitants of our house refuse to pull it out before they sit down. Instead, certain inhabitants — despite warnings from me — slide down the back, which weakens the chair. And since we only have four chairs, having one broken meant that either one person had to stand and eat or two people had to share a chair. Nobody wanted to do either, so we ended up eating in front of the TV in the living room — something I hate.

I sighed. With a little wood putty, carpenter's glue, and longer screws, the chair could be fixed. But chances were it wouldn't, any time soon, because if it isn't meowing or barking to be fed, clamoring for money or sitting in the car waiting to be driven to softball practice, it doesn't get any attention around our house.

That meant the broken chair would probably join the framed photo of Babe Ruth, which has been sitting on the dining room floor for the past three years waiting to be hung in the hallway.

Lord, this morning I left wanting to find Your glory, and I didn't. Will I ever find it? Surely, my home is not the place where it dwells!

As the plane crossed over from Georgia to Florida, I stared out the window and studied the houses down below. *My house is down there somewhere.*

As we passed over rural streets lined with citrus and pine trees, I recalled how sometimes when I see Laura pick up her baseball mitt or bat and I know she's on her way in the house to ask me to pitch to her, I'll pick up the phone and pretend I'm talking or else pretend I'm taking a nap — just to get out of playing ball with her.

I thought about how, when the girls were younger, I'd arrange the cards in Candyland so the game would end sooner or hide the Chutes and Ladders spinner to avoid playing altogether. Once I drove several miles out of the way to and from school for an entire week so I wouldn't have to pass a parking lot carnival. I didn't want to hear, "Mom, can we go? Can we go? Can we go?" and I didn't want to go.

No, my home can't be the place where Glory dwells.

As a flight attendant wheeled her beverage cart down the aisle, I overheard two young girls arguing in the seats behind me.

"You always get everything your own way!" screamed one.

"Well, you're just a baby!" yelled the other.

I cringed at the way their mother just sat there, doing nothing. It reminded me of my reaction to a recent fight I witnessed between my two girls. I was inside the hall closet scraping dried

I'm-not-sure-what off the carpeting and peeking through the lou-
vered slats in the door. I watched as Laura barged into the
bathroom and pushed past Alison to reach the box of hair ornaments, and I did nothing as Alison shoved Laura into the towel
bar. Laura shouted, "I hate you!" After that Alison slugged Laura
in the back and warned that if she told, she'd get in trouble for
hitting first.

The whole time I was in the closet I told myself, "You're the
mom. God has given you authority. They can't treat each other like
that — DO SOMETHING." But, I didn't do anything (except stay
hidden). I didn't want to deal with it. I didn't want to be the mom,
didn't want to impose penalties which too often punish me along
with them.

It's not possible that my home is the place where Glory dwells.
Is it?

I pondered the possibility, much as Floridians ponder the possibility of waking up to find snow on the front lawn. It's possible,
but how likely?

As we passed over a suburb north of Orlando, I pressed my
face against the window, wondering if we'd pass over my town,
my street, my house.

I picked out a white house with a big yard, pretended it was
mine, and imagined what might be going on inside. I had run
away from home. Of course, nobody knew. But still, by that time
the girls would have come home, and when they did, I wasn't
there. I hadn't even left a note.

I pictured both girls doing what they normally do: Laura
sprawled out on her back, feet on the wall, phone attached to her
head; Alison watching TV in the living room. Nothing spectacular, nothing out of the ordinary.

Except…from my new point of view two thousand feet above the earth, I saw beyond the ordinary. I saw life in progress. A house full of imperfection being perfected. Flaws being refined, character under construction, and patient endurance being tried and tested.

I saw Glory.

I rubbed my eyes and saw it again. Glory — dwelling in my home! — and it had been there all along.

In my home, the place where Glory dwells, cats claw at the furniture and bend the mini-blinds at the windows. Dried flower arrangements collect dust. Kids stuff candy wrappers in the couch cushions rather than throw them away. Lights and ceiling fans remain on. If a toothbrush falls on the bathroom floor, it often stays there for days before its owner picks it up.

In the place where Glory dwells, twelve-year-old girls emerge from their rooms wearing black lipstick, announcing they want to go to school "looking like death." Eight-year-olds pick locked bedroom doors and snoop through their sister's things. Ten-year-olds refuse to eat for a whole year and toddlers stuff grapes up their noses.

In the place where Glory dwells, the inhabitants rarely empty their pockets before throwing their clothes in the laundry and often end up with freshly laundered homework and/or shredded hockey tickets. The inhabitants burp in each other's faces and leave the toilet seats up. They eat spaghetti on the beds and lie about having done their homework. The inhabitants spend too much time in the shower and forget to turn the fan on — or off.

They forget their solemn vows to clean out the litter box daily and their promises to keep their rooms clean. They play with balls in the house (until something breaks) and step over the glob of spilled thousand island dressing on the kitchen floor rather than wipe it up.

In the place where Glory dwells, the inhabitants eat peanut butter and potato chip sandwiches and use licorice sticks as straws in their soda. They fight over the car radio stations and whose homework is harder, who's the bigger geek, and who did or did not eat the last of the ice cream.

In the place where Glory dwells, life is anything but glorious. It is selfish, not selfless; sinful, not holy. It is weak. It is cowardly, boastful, and rude. Yet, in spite of that, or maybe because of it, Glory set its sight on this very place, this very family.

Glory spoke, "I have loved you with an everlasting love," and came to dwell among us — we, the mess makers and promise breakers. We who go our own way and seek our own glory: we are the ones with whom Glory chose to dwell.

As the plane approached the landing strip in Orlando, I thought about what would happen when I got home. Most likely the girls would run out to ask where I'd been, what was for dinner, if Kelly could spend the night, if I could help with a humanities paper.

As I got off the plane and headed to the parking garage, I continued to think about home. This time, I thought about all the things Barry and the girls had done over the years to show me that they love me. Perhaps by the time I got home someone would have cleaned up the mustard or even vacuumed. Maybe someone would have started a load of laundry. Nothing spectacular, nothing too out of the ordinary.

Just a hint of Glory.

I thought about how later that night, when everyone was asleep, I would steal out from under Barry's arm, creep out of bed, and tiptoe through the house. In wonder and worship, I would walk on holy ground, awed by the Presence of Glory. Glory in my living room, with the ugly brown couch, dusty VCR and nail clippers left out on the coffee table. Glory in my kitchen where I struggle to make ground turkey taste like prime rib and sometimes sneak gulps of milk out of the carton in the fridge.

Glory underneath the roof that needs repair, where insults fly and sin is conceived.

Glory in my often cold and indifferent heart.

Not in a temple where all is perfect, not in a family without flaws, but with me, in my house, with my family.

By the time I reached my car, I felt as though I had been gone forever. So much had happened. I'd remembered all that I had forgotten about who I am as a wife and mother. I had discovered the place where Glory dwells. I even got an extra bag of honey roasted peanuts on the plane.

And so, with renewed diligence and an eagerness I didn't know I could possess, I fumbled through my purse for my keys....

I fumbled through my....

I fumbled....

I peered in my car window and spied my keys down by the brake pedal. Then I laughed.

This, too, is the place where Glory dwells.

"I love...the place where your glory dwells" (Psalm 26:8).